'This is a breathless and devastating re
intensity of a young woman who live(
fitting in, all the while documenting h~~c~~~~ ~~~~~~~~~~~~~~~~g~~ ~~
her writing and artwork. It is also a story of the strength of family love and in particular parents who both lay witness to and, with unwavering determination, try to ease the struggles their daughter experienced over years.

Colette's brutal and preventable death led the McCullochs on a new journey in search of answers and accountability. They were forced to negotiate a whole new world of coronial processes, obstruction and the contempt that families in such situations too often face. It is deeply saddening that bereaved families are subjected to consistently hostile and unnecessary treatment.

Why Can't You Hear Me? is, finally, an account of the immense losses that accompany the failing of health, social care and education systems to understand and recognise autism in girls and young women.

I wish I had met Colette. She was clearly a remarkable individual and this book speaks to her character, vivacity and life.'

– Sara Ryan, author of Justice for Laughing Boy

'This book is an emotional rallying call for changes in the way we respond to women with autism and mental ill-health. Colette, a talented artist and writer, conveyed her inner torment and needs but was not seen or heard by state agencies. Narrated by her loving family, it conveys their fight against a system that failed her, and them, in both life and death. In their pursuit of truth and accountability they have ensured Colette's creative free spirit lives on and we learn from her.'

– Deborah Coles, Director, INQUEST

'This poignant memoir of a young women born with autism spectrum disorder is a moving exemplification of the minds of others. Her parents use highly attuned empathy and biographical knowledge with insights from Colette's poetry in a compelling forensic analysis of her tragically short life story.'

– Janet Treasure, Professor of Psychiatry,
King's College London

Why Can't You Hear Me?

Our Autistic Daughter's Struggle to Be Understood

ANDY AND AMANDA
McCULLOCH

FOREWORDS BY JANE ASHER AND
PROFESSOR WILL MANDY

Jessica Kingsley Publishers
London and Philadelphia

First published in Great Britain in 2021 by Jessica Kingsley Publishers
An Hachette Company

1

Trigger Warning: This book mentions abusive/toxic relationship, alcohol, anxiety,
death, depression, eating disorders, abortion, self-harm, suicidal thoughts.

A CIP catalogue record for this title is available from the
British Library and the Library of Congress

ISBN 978 1 78775 508 6
eISBN 978 1 78775 509 3

Printed and bound in Great Britain by CPI Group

Jessica Kingsley Publishers' policy is to use papers that are natural,
renewable and recyclable products and made from wood grown in
sustainable forests. The logging and manufacturing processes are expected
to conform to the environmental regulations of the country of origin.

Jessica Kingsley Publishers
Carmelite House
50 Victoria Embankment
London EC4Y 0DZ

www.jkp.com

In memory of Colette Bianca McCulloch.

1981–2016

This book is for Colette, and in great part by Colette, in the hope that it may help other women and girls who live with autism.

Contents

Foreword by Jane Asher   11

Foreword by Professor Will Mandy   15

Authors' Note   17

Prologue   18

Part I

1. Ending   24

2. Follow the Yellow Brick Road   34

3. Moving On...   43

4. The Rolling Stones and GCSEs   50

5. Pathfinders in the Dark   60

6. Two As: A-Levels and Anorexia   65

7. A Life...?   75

Part II

8. Bethlem or Bedlam   80

9. A Creative Burst   88

10. Cry Freedom   96

11. The Umbilical Cord   104

12. Birkbeck: Vibrant Learning   113

13. The Undergraduate   124

14. Number Two, Hove   134

15. Online Fishing   143

Part III

16. The Void Beckons   152

17. All Change   164

18. The Law Is...   172

19. A Perfect Storm...   181

20. A Hard Place...   189

21. What Land Is This?   200

22. Milton Park: The Station to Nowhere   206

Part IV

23. Celebration and Confrontation   222

24. The Wheels of Justice   231

25. Letters Before Action   239

26. Action   248

27. Experts and Conclusions   261

28. Person Centred   273

29. Hope...   280

30. Beginning   287

Acknowledgements   291

Appendix   294

    Note to my Parents   294

    Shelf-Objects   298

    Broken Tea-Pot   300

Foreword

This book will break your heart – and if it doesn't it should. It reads like a Greek tragedy. We know the outcome from the start: indeed, the first chapter describes the terrible end of Colette's story in relentless, inexorable detail. Yet in this gripping, un-sensationalised account of her life and untimely death, we still hope for a different ending, unwilling to believe that the outcome for the intelligent, talented but troubled young woman we come to know through the pages of this beautifully written memoir will be to die alone on the A1, run over by a lorry in the middle of the night.

*   *   *

It must be over forty years since I went to a large children's charity tea party at the House of Commons to collect a cheque on behalf of Save the Children. Five other charities were also represented, and each had brought along a group of a dozen or so children to enjoy the fun. The children on one of these tables puzzled me: they didn't seem to be enjoying themselves and were unusually quiet – not interacting with each other, or chatting and shouting like those on the other tables, but seemingly each in their own world. I went over to talk to the smiling, kindly looking, middle-aged woman sitting with them. She introduced herself and explained that these were children with autism. I'd vaguely heard the term, but had no real idea of what it meant, or how it presented itself. Her explanation was detailed and fascinating, and I was intrigued. When, a few days after that introduction, I was approached to open a playgroup hosted by the National Autistic Society I jumped at it, and have been deeply enmeshed in the work of the society and the world of autism ever since.

It wasn't until later that I understood just how fortunate I was to have been given my introduction to this complex condition by Lorna Wing: one of the best-known and most highly respected figures working in psychiatry at that time, and a specialist in autism. Lorna, herself the mother of an autistic daughter, was the first to name the so-called 'triad of impairments', described to me at that time as problems with social interaction, social communication and lack of imagination.

It makes me cringe now to think of the way that in those days I would confidently stand up and talk about the condition – telling my audience that children with the condition would be unable to show emotion, had no creative or imaginative side and would be unlikely to learn to talk. We now know how wrong that was, even for those children who were severely affected. And as for the other end of the spectrum – it wasn't until the early nineties that I met Uta Frith, another brilliant expert in the field, who told me about the then recently named Asperger's syndrome and higher functioning autism. Around that time, so many clichés about autism began to be demolished, and as I learnt more and more it became clear just how impossible it was to generalise. As has been said many times, when you've met one person with autism, you've met...one person with autism.

One of the most upsetting features of Colette's story is that it wasn't until 2014 that her autism was diagnosed. Over the last ten years or so the difference between the way women/girls and their male counterparts present with autism has been recognised. Girls are better at disguising their lack of understanding of the neuro-typical world, smarter at covering up the behaviour that the rest of us would see as 'odd' and at hiding the angst and panic they may be feeling inside. It's unsurprising that anorexia is so strongly linked to autism – a condition that is all about exerting control could be irresistible to someone who lacks control in every other area, someone who has to live with the immense strain of pretending to be something she isn't in order to function. I think of one sweet girl with high functioning autism who will appear to have a different personality each time we meet; sometimes with a strong US accent, and at other times with a cute baby voice or perhaps appearing to be French. Being 'herself' is just too difficult.

Reading the book, it is humbling to see just how relentlessly Andy and Amanda, her devoted parents, battled for their beloved daughter all through her life, along with her equally loving sister, Chloe. And, cruelly, it's not just in Colette's lifetime that this battle took place: in this particular Greek tragedy there are villains that fill its pages after her death too. The unimaginable callousness of the coroner at the first inquest, the inhumanity of those responsible for her wellbeing at Milton Park who have never shown the slightest bit of remorse or been in touch since her death and the slow crawl of the system itself in the search for justice for Colette.

But what is equally shocking is the fact that through all the years of Colette being in the hands of countless medical and psychiatric experts and professionals, no one spotted the clues to her autism that now seem obvious. In some of the troubling

and heart-rending extracts from her diaries the words scream
out her condition:

> I couldn't comprehend the normality of those around me.
> What made them tick and how?
>
> I am never able to decipher facial expressions or subtle
> allusions to this or that. It makes me even more paranoid
> that I'm acting out of context.
>
> And do you know, I really cannot understand the
> language that you speak.

I am writing these words in the midst of the pandemic of 2020,
locked down like the rest of the country and unable to communicate in any normal, natural way with the rest of society.
Colette spent her entire life in lockdown, and if only the vital
key – her autism diagnosis – had been found earlier and this
lovely, creative girl been given the understanding and support
she needed, she might well have been with us still, living a life
of freedom and joy.

Jane Asher, actress, author and
President of the National Autistic Society

Foreword

Why Can't You Hear Me? is about the life and untimely death of Colette McCulloch, a woman of exceptional and singular creativity. The book has two authors – Colette's parents Andy and Amanda McCulloch. But there is a third voice that speaks throughout the text, that of Colette herself, expressed through her poetry and prose. She struggled to be heard and understood during her lifetime, but here her words are arresting and unambiguous.

Colette was autistic, but this was only recognised when she was thirty-three years old. By that point she had spent many years living with a state of despair. This partly came from a profound sense of unease she suffered as an undiagnosed autistic person in a world rigidly run by and for non-autistics. Even after she was recognised as autistic, despite the strenuous efforts of her family, she did not receive the care from professionals that she needed, and Colette died at the age of thirty-five in what was eventually described by her coroner as 'an avoidable tragedy'.

In my view, this book has several purposes. It is an act of grieving by two parents who have experienced an unimaginable tragedy. It is a conversation between those parents and their beloved daughter. And, also, the book is an invocation to health care professionals such as myself that we need to get better at recognising autistic people, and at properly supporting them in a world that is all too often a hostile environment for the neuro-diverse. Colette's story illustrates how autistic girls and women are especially likely to be overlooked, and to suffer as a result.

I think that things have improved since Colette was a child – there is now more awareness that autism is not just a male condition, and we are getting better at recognising autistic girls and women. However, there is still much progress to be made if we are to eliminate tragedies of the sort that befell Colette and her family. We must continue to improve recognition of autistic people, so they can get support and understanding. And we must get better at accepting and celebrating neurodiversity, so that the unique creativity and vitality of people like Colette can be expressed, heard, appreciated and enjoyed.

Will Mandy, Professor of Neurodevelopmental Psychology at University College London

Authors' Note

This book is the story of our younger daughter Colette's life; her struggles with dyslexia, mental health and autism, and the failing systems that were meant to support her. We include a lot of her poetry and prose. We've retained her text as she wrote it – the spelling and punctuation are her own and we have not corrected them. All the drawings and paintings in this book are by Colette.

The book has been edited in line with advice from relevant organisations on topics like self-harm and eating disorders. However, in order to find a balance between removing potentially triggering material and being true to Colette's, and our family's, experiences there are some passages which readers may find distressing. If so, we recommend contacting a resource such as the charity Beat, which provides support on these issues.

Prologue

Bethlem Hospital 30th March, 2003

Dear Mum,

I have done the painful part. I have been dragged slowly and unwillingly out of the nest Anorexia provides. I have reached the point that I feel more than aching bones and blue hands. Life is beckoning and I must make this final effort in order that I can live again.

It's a beautiful evening. The birds are chattering outside and, for a moment, I feel at peace. I imagine myself in a summer frock, sitting out on the patio, looking at the weeping willows and pondering the strangeness of things.

I hope that my 23rd birthday will be celebrated in style; out of hospital and living a life. Who knows where you and I will be a year from now! Who knows what script Dad might have written, what life I might be leading, what work you might be doing? Who knows? Time will tell.

Love as always - Col

That was Col in positive mode, aged twenty-two, anticipating leaving Bethlem Royal Hospital Eating Disorders Unit. Her default mode over the three years she'd been in and out of the unit is more truly expressed in her poem 'Note to my Parents' written less than a year earlier. This is the first verse:

> Would you believe me
> If I said that life has become
> Impossible?
> That your daughter feels she cannot
> Breathe the very air around her.
> That, to run a bath and wash
> Is too much effort of a will
> lost looking at a hat
> In the window of a pink shop.[1]

With benefit of hindsight, we realise Colette's autism had always been present in her behaviour, her writing, her artwork. However, it was twenty years ago; a different time. Autism was seen as a male condition. It wasn't looked for in girls. She was clearly suffering from the classic, anxious-girl's illness, anorexia. No need to look further. We now know 40% of anorexic girls may well be on the spectrum[2] but we didn't back at the turn of the century. The psychologist and nurse practitioner, who eventually diagnosed Col in 2014, producing a definitive Complex Case Review, read her poems and studied her paintings as a part of their assessment. The writing and art confirmed their findings

---

1   The full text of 'Note to my Parents' is in the Appendix.
2   Leake, J. (2019) 'Doctors "fail to spot autism" in thousands of girls.' *The Times*, 8 September.

that she had, in their words, 'High Functioning Autistic Spectrum Disorder'.

This book is an attempt to glimpse the appalling frustrations and pain she experienced throughout her life. Frustrations shared, to some extent, by most people on the spectrum.

Frustrations we shared during her life fighting for diagnoses, treatment and care. We spent years searching for the person, the doctor, the psychiatrist who could find the key and unlock the mind of our complicated daughter. A mind that could compose a beautiful, perceptive sonnet, that would break your heart. But could equally shout obscenities at us like an incandescent twelve-year-old.

After her death we perhaps came to empathise more with her frustrations as we struggled to expose the truth of how she was failed in her treatment. Bureaucratic, medical and legal doors were slammed in our faces. Her death was 'purely and simply a road accident, nothing more'. Forget the fact that she was resident in a mental health clinic/care home yet somehow she came to be walking on the A1 at 3 am! It was as if there was an establishment conspiracy saying, 'This person was not important enough to justify the expense of investigating her death.' This book is about how authority must always be questioned and how we must never accept convenient answers.

Above all, this book is about a free spirit. A genuinely funny, infuriating, challenging, unique and creative individual, who was literally and metaphorically crushed by our 'normal' world. But who in a better, more humane, existence could have flourished and left her mark. We will do this by describing her life through our memories. And through her own quirky, highly charged poetry, prose, short stories and art that she has left behind...

Col in spotty hat aged 18 months

Part I

CHAPTER 1

Ending

If only they knew,
Had any idea of what I am
And how much I need
To get out of here.
If only I could transmit it
To them, those hearts of cold stone.[1]

Milton Park Therapeutic Campus 27 July 2016

Yesterday you decided to colour your hair. You fancied auburn red – something striking for your move to the new placement. You tried a henna dye in the bath. It stung your body and splashed in your eye, you told us. You were scared that it might damage your sight. You wanted reassurance. You were always very concerned about your eyes. Years earlier Dave, your petty-criminal boyfriend in Brighton, had hit you hard across the face, hurting your eye. You screamed at him, called a cab and rushed to the Eye Hospital. You were terrified he'd damaged your retina. You were hysterical, ready to report the little shit to the police. When

---

1   Excerpt from 'The Tunnel' by Colette.

the hospital assured you that the eye wasn't damaged you were so relieved that you didn't even bother about the bruised cheek. Nor did you report your abuser; instead you let him back into your flat and your life.

Today the doctor tells you no harm has been done by the henna. You've put aside that worry and you're on your mobile.

'Hi Mum, I'm in my usual Costa café in Bedford.'

Why Costa? Because all Costas look exactly the same. You get exactly the same double espresso, in exactly the same cup. It's safe, you know where you are.

'I'm looking at people and I'm writing a short story Mum, then I'll go shopping.'

Books to read, clothes and bedding for what will be your new home. Waterstones and Primark? Will you have the money to pay for it all? Was it two or three days ago your card was refused at the cash machine? You reach for your mobile again.

'Dad...?'

He sighs and tells you that you took out your limit yesterday. You won't be able to get more cash till tomorrow. Just pay with the card. But you really should be thinking about getting a bus back to Milton Park now – you've been out longer than your four-hour limit already. Boring! You end the call.

You don't want to go back, not yet. You're not looking forward to the new place either. It may be even worse. It's not fair. Why can't you just live in a Premier Inn? Any Premier Inn – they're all the same, like Costa you know where you are.

Mum phones you later, it's evening now. You tell her about the books you bought and how you've seen some really sexy tops at Primark. You want reassurance about them. You love it when Mum gets in a tizz about your clothes being too sexy. You feel comforted – she cares. You've bought them anyway. Once you've decided something, that's it, you have to do it. Mum wants you to go back to Pathway House (part of Milton Park Campus, where you're being treated) now you've done your shopping.

'I can't Mum, I've met a guy called James and we're in a pub. He's got a pedigree dog. I'm helping look after it.'

'It's getting late darling, it's half past eight, you mustn't miss the last bus.'

You will go back, but you're not ready yet. It's a lovely sunny summer evening...

Amanda and I were preparing to go away for a few days before Colette's move from Pathway House. She had a new placement in an NHS clinic/care home in her home county of Sussex. We had high hopes of this clinic/care home, though we knew any change was hard for Col. She said she didn't want to see us till she'd made the move. Her gig. We agreed. We had warned staff that her anxiety levels would escalate as the date of the move approached. Even though she hated Milton Park, moving was still very scary for her. Given her state, we were surprised the clinic/care home gave her leave to go the ten miles into Bedford.

It was now 9.30 pm. We'd tried calling a couple more times, you hadn't picked up. We tried again. This time you answered. James could be heard, shouting, in the background. He was clearly inebriated.

'Col you must leave now or you'll miss the last bus.'

'I'll make my own arrangements. I know what I'm doing Dad.'

'Whatever you do Col, don't get into a car with that man. He is too drunk to drive.'

You ended the call. It was the last time we talked to you.

By now we were getting extremely worried. We phoned Pathway House. We pointed out that she had been out for over twelve hours now. The support worker, Danielle, said she'd been in contact with Col and she'd said she'd come back on the next bus. But she hadn't. We told Danielle that she ought to contact the police. She was reluctant to do so. Bedfordshire Police had given the clinic/care home a designated ID code for reporting when Colette went missing. (It had happened a number of times before, and they usually found her.) Danielle said she'd give her a bit more time before taking any action. She would call us as soon as she heard anything.

Nothing. Phone silence. 11 pm. Once again I rang Danielle: 'It's very late Danielle, you must alert the police now.'

'I've spoken to Colette and she says she's getting a taxi. If she's not back by 1 am I will call them.'

'1 am!? That's far too late Danielle!'

Danielle didn't call the police until 2 am – 17 hours after Col had left Pathway House. We will never understand why this support worker did not follow the agreed safety procedures that were put in place for Colette. We put the phone down. Bedford is over 65 miles away. We don't have a car. There was nothing we could do.

How you travelled the ten miles from Bedford to the A1 near Milton Park remains uncertain. You must have been caught on CCTV somewhere in Bedford with James and his dog. But the police never located any footage. The police are under-resourced and I doubt if they ever made a serious attempt to track down the CCTV. After all, the girl was dead and no crime had been committed. They did check the local taxi firms and none had any record of carrying you that night. Our own theory is that you persuaded James to give you a lift back. In the dark he could have missed the turning into the narrow lane that led to Milton Park. Probably running out of patience, he dropped you off on the A1 to walk from there. James hasn't been identified so we will never know. The next definite reports of you come from police witness accounts. These are the relevant excerpts from one of their statements to the coroner's court:

> The A1 is a large dual carriageway with a 70mph speed limit... As I made my way down the verge I saw a white van pull to a stop on the Southbound carriageway. A person got out of the vehicle... I crossed to the central reservation of the A1 and he shouted the words to the effect of 'There is a woman in lane one. I nearly hit her. She's going to get killed.' I replied 'On the southbound side?' He replied 'Yes. About 500 yards back...'

The A1 at Eaton Socon is a bleak unlit tarmac expressway. There is no provision for pedestrians. What was going through your mind as you strode determinedly along the carriageway ignoring the fast-moving traffic? Had you had a row with James? Had he thrown you out of the car? If this were a novel, it would describe your emotions, your thoughts, at this moment. Blind fury at the injustice of the world? Frustration and anger that you somehow could never be free? That they, the doctors, the nurses, the therapists, weren't listening to you but were instead intent on controlling your every movement? A feeling of 'Fuck it! Fuck you all! Do your worst!' perhaps? We'll never know for sure but it seems quite likely. Sadly, though, this is not a novel, it's a factual account of events leading to an avoidable tragedy. PC Finn's report continues:

> At this point I realised there was a very real and immediate threat to the life of this person...and any other road users on the A1... I began to run along the central reservation of the A1 in the direction the van driver had told me... A number of police vehicles passed us on the Northbound carriageway and I heard PC 6202 Bowles call up on the radio and say that there was a female on the Southbound carriageway who had been hit by a lorry...

The police had by now stopped the traffic. PC Finn continues:

> ... I made my way towards the body. I believed I recognised the
> female to be Colette McCulloch. I would describe her as aged
> approximately 30 years old, female, white and around 5 feet
> tall. I would describe her as wearing dark coloured clothing with
> long dyed dark red hair. She was lying with her head facing
> upwards and her body twisted. There was a large amount of
> blood around her head and on the ground. I have met Colette
> before and I believed it to be her however I could not be 100%
> sure as it was dark and her face was partially obscured by blood
> and hair. SPC Spenceley and I began to conduct an initial survey
> and check McCulloch for any vital signs such as breathing and
> a pulse. We were not able to find any signs of life however her
> body was still warm. She appeared to have a severe injury to
> the rear of her head. As we were doing this, a paramedic first
> responder arrived at scene and instructed us to begin CPR. PC
> 6207 Cannon, PC Marfell, SPC Spenceley and I all took turns
> performing chest compressions on McCulloch. This did not
> appear to be having any impact. A number of other medical
> staff arrived and took over treatment. At approximately 03:25,
> the medical staff on scene agreed that there was nothing more
> that could be done and pronounced death.

Seven am later that morning, in London, making coffee before
calling Pathway House to check that Col was safely back, a faint
ping. 'That the doorbell?' I ask. 'Bit early for the post.' Amanda
heads for the door.

I can glimpse from the kitchen the blue uniform of a male
cop. Amanda explains to him that we are about to leave for the
station but he insists on coming in. I go numb, somewhere I know
what this means.

He asks us to sit at the table. This is clearly not a part of the job he is at ease with. He proceeds to inexpertly blurt out his brutal message: 'Are you Andrew and Amanda McCulloch?'

We murmur affirmative answers.

'Are you the parents of Colette Bianca McCulloch of Milton Park?'

We barely whisper, yes.

'I have to inform you that your daughter was run over and died at 3 am this morning.'

An awful silence then Colette Bianca's parents cling to each other sobbing. The rest is a dreadful aching blank. And a persistent recurring sense of guilt – initial crazy guilt that if I hadn't asked Amanda to answer the door, Colette would somehow still be alive... Then the sickening realisation that she was dead. Tragedies that are reported in newspapers. Tragedies that only happen to other people, had happened to our daughter. Why did we ever allow her to be sent to that place...?

We had a great friend, Des, staying in our spare room. He was to house sit for the few days we were planning to be away. He came downstairs unaware of the tragedy that had taken place. Des is an incredibly sensitive guy and knew Colette well. He quickly absorbed the terrible truth. We can't remember what he said but it was comforting. A few days later he wrote a very moving poem, titled 'For Colette', which he sent to us.[2] Finally he said he thought he ought to leave us and give us space. He was quite right. We were in shock and we had all the formalities of death to negotiate. We had to identify her body the next morning.

I kept an erratic journal of my thoughts and feelings at this time. I think I saw it as therapy. Months later when I saw a bereavement counsellor, he encouraged me to write to Colette

---

2   Des McAleer's poem 'For Colette' is in Chapter 30.

as though we were having a correspondence. I suspect this was an unschooled attempt to do something similar. These are my first couple of entries exactly as I put them down:

> **Day One – 28 July 2016:** What am I doing trying to write down my feelings at a time like this? I'm a writer, of sorts, so am attempting to do something clever. Something that hasn't been done before. That breaks new ground. Something just plain bloody self-interested?
>
> My younger daughter has just been killed in a senseless road traffic accident. And all I can do is put down meaningless words onto a computer!
>
> **Day Two – 29 July:** On auto-pilot. Train to St Neots to identify her body. Cannot believe this is happening. Will it be better once we have witnessed her corpse? No idea.
>
> The thought of viewing her lying on the slab is disturbing. How badly damaged will she be? They say she's not bad. The truck hit the back of her head, not her face.

PC James Styles, late thirties, above medium height, with a friendly demeanour but tired eyes, is on the platform as Amanda and I get off the train. His patrol car is parked outside with his colleague, an older male special constable, at the wheel. They are to be our guides and companions for the emotionally stressful day. In contrast to the poor guy who broke the news to us in London, these two do an excellent job.

Colette was in the mortuary of Addenbrooke's Hospital outside Cambridge. The drive from St Neots Station takes some time. The cops keep up a respectful but easy conversation, or 'convo' as Col would have called it. We hear how the traffic police in the Beds, Cambs, Herts forces have been cut from six patrol cars to three. How three forces had been combined into one, meaning long drives from Luton to Peterborough, etc. How 35% of their workload now is dealing with MH (mental health) cases and that they aren't trained for that.

All this time Amanda and I sit in the back, numb. We can't envisage the encounter to come. What state would her body be in? Would she be recognisable? We know the lorry had hit her from behind, would her skull be caved in?

The car slows. A large glass and concrete structure, all towers and low-rise buildings, looms up out of the flat Cambridgeshire landscape. 'This is us,' says PC Styles calmly. The hospital is vast, modern and impersonal. The cops lead us through a labyrinth of passageways till we eventually reach a waiting area outside the mortuary. PC Styles asks us if we were okay to see her now. We nod that we are. He opens the door and we go in. He follows us.

She's lying on more of a bed than a slab. Amanda and I stare at her. Her eyes have been closed. She's lying on her back, her mouth closed.

'But...she looks asleep. Is she just in a coma?' Amanda whispers.

'No, I'm sorry, she's dead. Touch her,' PC Styles gently corrects.

We put our hands on her face and kiss her. She's stone cold. She must be room temperature but she feels much colder. There is no sign of the traumatic head injury that killed her, just a cut on the side of her face. They've cleaned her up well. We start talking to her quietly. We cry and hold each other.

We go to the door and turn round for one last look. It's so strange. She really does look as though she's in a light sleep, about to wake up and ask us to get her out of here. She always hated hospitals. Ironic given how much of her short life was spent in them...

Madness began last night
And has followed me into the day.
Now I feel helpless. Nowhere to turn.
You know when you've opened madness's
Door, because your mind stops looking
For the living alternatives.
It sees, now, there might not be one
On this earth.[3]

---

3   From 'The Tunnel' by Colette.

CHAPTER 2

Follow the Yellow Brick Road

'I wan Widerozz! I wan Widerozz!' 2 am. The little girl is running up and down the long living room.

She stops and points to the TV screen. The mother wearily clicks on the VHS video again. The screen lights up with Dorothy, the Cowardly Lion, the Tin Man, the Scarecrow and the Munchkins singing and dancing, weaving their magic web. The little girl is transfixed. Eyes glued to the screen, she starts to dance, munchkin-like, to the music.

Dee dah, dee dah, dee dah dah,

Dee dididy dah dee dah

The following night the father is on the sofa with the child. 'I wan Widerozz, I wan Widerozz.'

A deep sigh,

'Oh Colette, not again. The same film over and over. It's getting really boring.'

'I wan Widerozz, Widerozz, Widerozz!'

He gives in and shoves the video into the machine. He nods off into an uneasy slumber. The catchy upbeat music and singing, from the video, echo round his semi-conscious brain. A sudden sharp pain in his ribs. He wakes with a start to realise that his toddler daughter is jabbing him with her elbow, a huge grin across her face. She points to the screen where Dorothy and the Scarecrow cavort and sing. She proclaims with a mischievous laugh, 'It's really boring.'

Were you still two or were you three when this particular obsession started? We didn't think of it as an obsession of course. It was just another of our younger daughter's eccentricities.

When you were two-and-a-half we went on holiday to France. We were renting a friend's house which was quite small and the only people there were us and your sister Chloe. The weather was very hot and you were, as usual, not sleeping much. You would stand up in your travel cot chanting, 'Home...home...home.'

One night you got up, put on your mother's high heels and tottered up the village street. Startled villagers watched, amused to see us pursue our naked toddler, in high heels, running down the street. French opinions about how weird Les Anglais are were instantly confirmed.

What became clear is that from an early age you needed the reassurance of the familiar. You had boundless energy. Amanda used to take you to two playgroups a day and still you wouldn't sleep. Chloe was five years older. Exhausted from school, she would be in bed asleep by 7.30 pm. If we were lucky you were asleep by 2.30 am.

Back home, friends come round to supper in the red tiled kitchen. We all sit round our old pine table. You sit to one side at your own little red table and chair. You run in and out fetching and playing with various toys, completely absorbed. 'We cannot get her to stay in bed,' we explain, 'just doesn't work.' Friends laugh and say she's extraordinary!

On the surface you appeared to be a happy, carefree child.

However, we suspect now that the warning signs of unease were there, we just didn't read them. Years later, in your early twenties, when an inpatient at the Bethlem Royal Hospital, you would set out to write what you termed as your autobiography. Early in the book you write:

> How shall I start this narrative of myself? In what way can I, author, convey to you, reader, what my life was like before this affliction.
> I was happy. I realise that now, for I know it to be the antithesis of my current feelings.
> All the photographs show it. The smile. The raised left finger, characteristic of my youth.
> I was vivacious. I was outgoing and excitable and all-embracing. I loved life and I believed that life loved me. On entering a crowded room, I was looked at. Taken notice of, because of what I gave out. Because I was me and comfortable with it and because life was weird and wonderful and the intensity of my gaze translated all this, dear reader, to any casual observer.[1]

You were on the borderline of being hyperactive but otherwise a normal happy child, our GP said when we consulted her about the not sleeping. The first of many diagnoses. It seemed about right to us but none of us were close to realising that something much deeper was going on. Our GP said, 'She'll probably grow out of it once she's at primary school.'

Honeywell Primary School was, while being housed in a large Victorian building, a friendly place. The headmistress was old school, with a ginny baritone voice, but many of the teachers

---

1   From Colette's autobiography.

were young and committed. Chloe, your older sister, given a few blips, got on well there and made a lot of friends. You were initially fine. But, unlike Chloe, you didn't make many friends. In fact, you only really had one – Susana. You were extremely close, from ages six to eight. You were almost inseparable. Susana was very bright, an only child living with her single-parent mother. She was often looked after by her grandparents who were old and not very well. She found refuge in books. You adored her. You wrote about her years later:

> There was magic everywhere in Susana's world, as there was in mine I've never met another kindred spirit since... One afternoon in the park, Susana and I discovered large balls of coal... This fairly normal incident, nevertheless, was fuel enough for my imagination.
> The coals are hot. 'Yes, they are, Susana. Do not doubt it. Pick one up and Aslan will never let you enter Narnia!' Narnia. Susana read all the Narnia books. Devoured them one by one and when she'd finished, she'd start from the beginning again.
> It didn't seem fair that I, the story - teller in the relationship, could not share Susana's delight on opening a volume of C. S Lewis and be transported to that other, enchanting, mystical world!

When you were seven years old something happened in class. It changed everything for you. The teacher was handing a *Janet and John* book round for pupils to read out loud in turn. For some reason, she had to step outside the classroom for a brief word with a colleague. The book was passed on to you.

On returning, the teacher was surprised to hear gales of laughter in her class. She stepped in to hear you in full voice describing how Janet and John were flying through the air, high above the houses, holding onto a magic giant panda.

That evening there was a phone call. 'Mrs McCulloch... I have tell you that I don't think Colette can read a word... She's just making up stories.'

Drawing of 'Carrallnes Invencher'

Now the world of school became a hostile environment, for you. Enemy territory. Where there had been joy and creativity, now there was fear and shame. As you wrote in your autobiography years later:

> I concentrated hard. Chisselled a hole in the blackboard on which my eyes would transfix, as though some Holy-Grail presided there. But it didn't work, and I was found-out. Pushed to the front of the classroom, where the 'thick dunces' sat...
> But Miss Piercy never forgave me my seeming stupidity. My mind's inability to conform to the norms of curricular learning. After school I was kept back to talk to her...

My recollections of her lecture pivot around the word 'stupid'. A big, loaded, daemon-faced word!! The word was blistered on my thoughts; 'Stupid!!'

And if I were to divide my life in to the 'happy' and the 'not so happy', then the 'not so happy' would begin at the diagnosis of dyslexia... It was this devastating revelation that left me trembling with fear. So there was something wrong with me. I wasn't quite normal. I didn't quite 'fi t' like everyone else did.

Reading this now we can see how alienated from the neuro-typical world you felt but at the time we were baffled. You were articulate for your age. You enjoyed using words. 'Could she be dyslexic?' we asked. At that time the term dyslexia was not widely accepted by many teachers. It was seen as an attempt by middle-class parents to say their child wasn't thick when they couldn't read. The deputy head was a paid-up dyslexia denier and said Colette would have to go into a special remedial class once a week. Once a week? We knew that would not solve the problem. We sought a second opinion.

The dyslexic experts we consulted both carried out full appraisals. In their opinion Colette had an above-average IQ but was severely dyslexic. They recommended specialist teaching:

Children with dyslexia usually appear bright, intelligent, and articulate but are unable to read, write, or spell at an age-appropriate level. They will generally have average or above average intelligence, yet may have poor academic achievement. They may have good oral language abilities but will perform much more poorly on similar written-language tests. They might be labelled lazy, dumb, careless, immature, 'not trying hard enough', or as having a 'behaviour problem'.

In a way we were relieved. Now at least we thought we knew what we were dealing with. That unfortunately turned out to be far from the reality. You reacted really badly to the diagnosis. You felt labelled by it. Dyslexic! Stupid! Not quite normal! You started to eat for comfort. You put on weight. This made you even more unhappy, and the bullying began. 'Collywobble, Fatso, chub-chub.' Weight became a constant source of anxiety.

At school, a playground game had been instigated by the gym instructor: The Piggy Back Game. A group of kids make a circle, another group walk around it. When the whistle blows you have to jump on the back of the nearest kid and see how long they can carry you.

> Need I explain that I hated this game? That I had nightmare after nightmare about all the potential devastating scenarios... I had the added misfortune of always ending up having to piggy back on a boy. When a girl dropped me it was understandable. But if a boy couldn't even sustain my bulk?! It makes my cheeks burn to remember!![2]

By complete chance a specialist dyslexic school, Hornsby House, opened within walking distance of our house in Clapham. Dr Beve Hornsby, who founded the school, was one of the world's leading experts in dyslexia. You went there for just over a year; four full terms. There were only seven pupils in a class, they taught phonetics and you learned to read fluently in a matter of months. But Hornsby House only took kids through to 11 years old. You had to move on, so for your last year before secondary school we took you back to Honeywell Primary School so that you could move back into the state system.

---

2   From one of Col's diaries.

Now, installed at Honeywell once again, instead of being seen as lazy, dumb and careless, you were top of the class in everything, except the dreaded maths.

Strange-scented mornings;
Peace of mind on Saturdays.
The clock ticking comfort
On a shelf
Above the bed, or was it
Near the window? ...
Pink glow of Autumn,
Wellingtons and Piles
Of leaves. Orange Streets
And conckers.
Mum wore picksy boots
With pointy toes
And laces. Too much
Eye-line even then.
A tiny wrinkled hand
In mine; 'Kitchen Hands'
She always said,
And I laughed, never
Thinking I would one day
Have the same,
And at a younger age.
I'd press the ball of
Her thumb, feel the
Hardened skin collapse
Beneath my pressure;
Like air-pop wrapping
Used for delicate things;
Like mum.[3]

---

3   From 'Shelf-Objects' written in 2003 – full text in the Appendix.

With your new-found confidence, you did well in class. Mission accomplished, it might seem. You read books above your age range. You wrote for pleasure. But there remained a serious downside. You had few friends. While you were away from Honeywell, your soulmate Susana had moved to California with her mother. You were devastated by her absence. Most of the other kids at Honeywell shunned you. They knew you'd gone away because you couldn't read. You were right, they saw you as being a bit weird.

Because I understood in the playground, surrounded by bunches and huddles of friends I couldn't join in, what it was to be an outsider. Alone, and feeling so, so different.[4]

Gradually however you established one friendship with a girl who had been close with Susana as well. While you blamed us for the dyslexic label that you felt dogged you, you did grudgingly admit that the change of school had helped. Because of Hornsby House you could now read and write confidently. However, your dread of being 'different' had not been lessened.

Dyslexia had knocked your self-confidence in a profound way. For the rest of your life you would seek reassurance. You needed praise and confirmation of your abilities. You were terrified people would think you were stupid. Fat equals thick, thin equals clever. It never left you. We hoped when you went on to secondary school these fears would leave you and fade away.

---

4   From one of Col's diaries.

CHAPTER 3

Moving On...

'Good morning gels. Welcome to Lady Margaret School. I have to tell you first that there will be no more primary-school mollycoddling here. We will not tolerate lateness, homework must be in on time, laziness will not be accepted. I anticipate you all going on to excel in the world as previous Lady Margaret Gels have before you.'

Turned out in a neat twinset with carefully coiffed hair and make-up headmistress, Joan Olivier, might have been written by Muriel Spark. Jean Brodie to a T. She spoke in a cultured Morningside accent. She would refer to the pupils as her 'Gels'. She must have cut an alien figure to the millennial Fulham girls she was addressing. Most soon dismissed her as some relic from a bygone age. But her words and their ramifications struck fear into Colette.

Lady Margaret School is an all-girls comprehensive in Parsons Green, south-west London. We had chosen the school because it was small by London secondary standards, only four-hundred-and-fifty girls. We knew Col found large buildings confusing and would often lose her way in them. She also found places with a lot of people overwhelming. We hadn't wanted a single-sex school for her but on balance we felt a manageable caring environment was a safer choice than the 1,200-pupil comprehensive her older sister Chloe was in. It was a reasonable punt and who knows if any other choice would have been any better for her?

We had talked to the deputy head before term started and explained to him about her dyslexia. We asked him to alert the teachers but for them not to mention it in class. It remained a very sensitive subject for Col. She had largely come to terms with it but her spelling was still a bit eccentric. It was just something for staff to be aware of. So could it be kept confidential while making some allowance for her? He agreed.

Her English teacher could have been written by Charles Dickens rather than Muriel Spark. In late middle age, he was balding, overweight with waistcoats that he was bursting out of. He was in many ways a good teacher and loved literature; a genuine expert on the works of Jane Austen. But he had a penchant for picking on certain girls, making them stand on a table and recite poems. It was embarrassing and humiliating and they hated it. He left later, after complaints from parents.

However, what he did to Colette was in many ways worse than making her stand on a table. He was of course a dyslexia denier. On reading the notes on the intake of his new class he stood and took in the sea of young faces: 'Apparently there's a girl in this class who suffers from dyslexia – would she please stand up?!'

Silence.

'Come along, young lady you must know who you are.'

He looked searchingly in the direction of the terrified Colette. At least she thought he was looking at her she told us later. Eventually she felt forced to stand. He then rubbished the diagnosis of dyslexia saying the condition didn't exist. She went bright red; she was shamed in front of the whole class. Devastated she understandably blamed us for telling the deputy head – now everybody in the school knew she was different.

I hated myself from the age, approx, of eleven. It never got better.

Line drawing aged 11

Other unforeseen problems with going to Lady M soon emerged as well. Colette had to take a train from Clapham Junction then change at Wimbledon, to get to Parson's Green. She'd never had a great sense of direction and frequently ended up on the wrong train.

'Dad I'm in a phone box... I don't know where I am. I'm going to be late Dad. What am I going to do?'

'It's alright Col. Where are you?'

'I don't know Dad, but I can see some cows in a field.'

She'd somehow got on the wrong train and ended up in Surrey...

One of us would jump in the car, collect her and deliver her to school.

She would often get lost in the school itself, despite it being quite small. She seemed unable to retain any directions given to her. She was always doing the wrong homework because she hadn't taken in the teacher's instructions. She drove some staff members to distraction, asking them to confirm what they'd already told her. Even then she couldn't remember what they'd said. All these 'failings' led to being kept back for detentions. Once again she felt shamed – thick, useless, stupid. Fat!

Fat, she wasn't in reality. We have photographs of her just before she went to secondary school, when she was a bridesmaid. She looks great. A huge smile on her face, beaming at the bride. A month later her first term started at her new school.

Moving from primary school to secondary can be traumatic for many kids. For Colette it was catastrophic. The very first term she lost a lot of weight. Her uniform was falling off her. Amanda had to take in her skirt twice that term alone. We thought it was just down to stress with all the homework, the journey, etc. We hoped things would settle down.

> A fat girl with a sad face,
> her eyes full of remorse,
> each photo of that long ago
> I ripped to bits of course.
> Unhappy lived inside that girl,
> it had become her friend,
> and yet I later came to know
> on this you can't depend.

But now the problems were piling up. Discipline was maintained at Lady M's through detentions after school. Col was frequently late, did the wrong homework, forgot which class she should be in. Detention, detention, detention. Stupid, stupid, stupid. She felt shamed each time she was kept back and her friends went cheerfully home. Her mood became increasingly anxious and depressed. Sunday nights were worst as she contemplated another Monday. She withdrew into herself.

The girl could not shrug off the feeling,
it was nested in her fat,
so all that she could ever do
was lose it and be flat.
But unhappy she still lived within,
it was bedded in her soul,
I thought that it was in my flesh
nature had taken its toll.

She started to avoid food. At supper, she'd say she was frightened the food on our plates might jump up into her mouth. She went from being a relatively carefree, often cheeky child to being miserable most of the time. The weight loss continued. Sometimes she would stare at our wooden kitchen table and scream. She'd seen a food stain on it. 'It's going to jump into me!' she'd yell.

One night she refused to eat anything except yoghourt. We didn't have any. It was 9 pm. I drove to the nearest convenience store and bought her some. She was standing on the stairs when I got back. She took off the lid, took one mouthful then spat it out screaming, 'It's got bits in it!' We were very disturbed. Where had our daughter gone? It was as though she was possessed.

No laughing and no cheerful smiles,
unhappy had already won,
perhaps I could be normal again
but the damage had been done.
I stood in front of my mirror,
I smiled at what I saw.
A skeleton stared back at me,
this was good for sure.[1]

---

1 'Unhappy' by Colette, aged twelve.

At thirteen she was diagnosed with obsessive compulsive disorder (OCD) and was sent to an adolescent unit. We agreed to her going there for three weeks of analysis. The child psychiatrist was sympathetic and seemed kind. He said the referral was essential. He thought her OCD needed treatment before it took hold.

Woodside Adolescent Unit turned out to be a dismal building. Colette was young to be admitted. We were very uncertain about the placement.

The stay at Woodside did initially seem to have helped. Some weeks after coming home Col started to eat. She gained some weight and looked much healthier. She interacted with girls from school once more. Her moods lifted. There was laughter in the house again. We held our breath...

But, in fact, her admission to Woodside had only identified a small part of her condition. It was as though they had sighted an iceberg and, knowing nothing about arctic ice flows, had assumed what they saw above the surface was the totality. They were unaware of the 90% of the ice that was concealed; unaware of the real mental distress that was driving her. There were no follow-up appointments with child psychiatry. No monitoring of her state of mental health. A treatment box had been ticked and that was it. But Col's demons remained unidentified, only to re-emerge with a vengeance as GCSEs loomed on the horizon.

> I don't know where I'll be next year,
> it seems so far away,
> I'm walking down this lonely road
> frightened I may stray.
> Voices ringing in my ears
> pushing me to move.
> I don't know where I'll be next year,
> I've got so much to prove.

I'm drowning in this turbulent sea,
there's nothing to grab onto,
and there they all are mocking me
laughing at my misfortune
I wish that I were five years old
with nothing to care about,
I wish that I was young again
allowed to scream and shout.
I don't know where I'll be next year,
I haven't got a clue.
The thing that makes it sadder is
It all ends up on you.[2]

---

2 'Next Year' by Colette, aged fourteen.

CHAPTER 4

The Rolling Stones and GCSEs

Mick Jagger sketch by Colette

Until now you hadn't shown any special interest in music of any sort. You liked dancing and would often sing loudly when sitting on the loo. Exactly why you were so drawn to The Rolling Stones was something of a mystery. Surely Oasis, Blur or Supergrass, rather than a bunch of grandads? However, you were soon spending all your pocket money on their CDs and books about the band. You talked about them incessantly.

'Did you know Dad that Mick and Keith re-met on Dartford

Station in 1961? But it was Brian Jones who started the band. And Andrew Loog Oldham created their image. He made them dangerous, the kind of boys no dad wants his daughter to go out with.'

'Maybe. But the Jagger and Richards chemistry is what mattered,' I countered.

'Brian was the main man, Dad, when they kicked off,' you corrected me. 'He decided on their name and their gigs. And he was the sexiest.'

With that you waltzed up to your room to play the latest CD at full volume. Years later, in your autobiography, you remember this obsession with remarkable clarity:

> I love it. Just sitting there; immersed in capturing the essence of the person on my paper. The pencil darting forth, the pondering on detail, with precision and loving care. I listened to old Rolling Stone tracks as I drew - 'Ruby Tuesday', 'Paint It Black', 'She's Like a Rainbow'. It was magical, because when I was deep in the contemplation of these mysterious icons I became a part of them. They became my friends.
> I think mum and dad thought it quite extraordinary really. I think they liked the opportunity to take out their musty 60s photos and show me how ridiculous, reckless and happy they were.[1]

Woodside had really scared you. We'd soon realised it was not the right place for you. We'd thought there would be treatment for your OCD but there seemed to be precious little. Three weeks after your admission you were discharged and came home. You

---

1   From Col's autobiography.

vowed that you'd never be sent there again. You started to eat more normally. You gained a bit of weight. Your moods lifted. Back at school with a new English teacher, Mr Winterflood, whom you liked, you wrote a short story based on your time at the adolescent unit.

It was about your friendship with your roommate in the unit, a girl called Vicky. It was a vivid tale. A mixture of fact and fiction. Vicky was charismatic and self-destructive. You were in awe of her.

There was one particularly grey morning, when the skies lay heavy and low with the weight of their drink, that me and Vicky made a unanimous decision... 'You in the mood for something fun', she enquired whilst blackening her eyes with a thick, clumsy pencil. In my usual position on my bed I then sat up and looked at her questioningly. 'There's a forest but half a mile from here. Its forbidden for anyone to set foot in the place, ever since the mysterious death of the little choir boy. The trees beckon me to go, they're calling me right now, screaming for me as he once screamed on that bloody afternoon. The doctors and nurses claim that I'm mad when I speak in this way, do you agree.' She turned to face me and never before have I seen such deadened eyes, like the very pupils were blocks of ice...[2]

The gothic-style fantasy was about how the two roommates escaped, through a window, into the grounds in the middle of the night. Their adventure was scary and surprising. The story genuinely flew off the page and the ending was quite moving. Mr

---

2   From 'Reminiscence', a short story by Colette, aged fourteen.

Winterflood, your teacher, was deeply impressed by the writing. You came home really chuffed by his reaction. You reported to us what he'd said.

'That's an extraordinary story Colette. What made you think of it? Has anything like that ever happened to you?'

'Not exactly. Vicky was based on a real person. But the adventure was in my imagination.'

'Amazing. Perhaps you'll become a writer one day.'

When we talked to Mr Winterflood, to tell him of your death years later, he remembered that story. He'd never forgotten it. He had had great hopes for you. He was devastated by the news we gave him.

'Mr Winty's' reaction to your writing, at the time, meant a lot to you. You blossomed. You made a few friends at school. You even asked two of them to come on holiday with us in the summer. We had renovated a derelict cottage in south-west France a few years earlier. We now spent all our holidays there. We held family events like my mother's eightieth birthday party there, where you met and engaged with cousins and friends alike. One boy became the object of your schoolgirl crush. You wrote about him years later in your autobiography:

Dominic and I slouched on the sofa. The photos I proudly displayed to my friends, later, when I realised nothing could or would come of it.
He was beautiful. Was everything I could desire.
The olive skin I touched, soft cheek, warm finger - tips.
I liked his neck the most. His neck and the captivating features of his face.

You continued to place Dominic on a pedestal for some years. Being at an all-girls school meant that you had a rose-tinted view of boys. But during the holidays in France you met both French and English boys and they mingled freely – all very easy-going and relaxed. Each village had its own fete – music, wine, food, dancing, clowns and acrobats. The atmosphere was great, hippy and fun. Local teenagers and foreign holidaymakers all joined in. However, despite your first name, you found French very difficult. Coping with dyslexia in your own language is one thing; in a foreign language it's another. You always got poor marks in tests. You found it annoying, especially because your mother spoke it so well.

But French boys now supplied the incentive for some serious holiday work to improve your language skills. The summer before GCSEs we were in France as usual. On one of your long walks together, you asked your mother to help you prepare for your French oral exam.

'I need to be able to say my name Mum, where I'm from and what hobbies I have.'

'No problem, just say *"Je m'appelle Colette. J'habite à Londres et quand je dessine tous mes soucis disparaissent."'*

It was true your worries did disappear when you drew. You repeated this many times. The next evening was the start of the biggest local fete. We were sitting on a wall having a beer when you came rushing up to us. Amanda takes up the story.

'Mum, Mum. I've got to get away, quick, quick!'

She propelled me up the hill towards the food stalls and the tents where all the 'spectacles' were happening.

'Honestly Mum, you are hopeless. What a ridiculous phrase you've taught me.'

'Why Col, what's happened?'

'A French boy came up to me and asked me my name, I replied *"Je m'appelle Colette."* Then he said something else so I went, *"Quand je dessine tous mes soucis disparaissent."* And then he started jabbering away at me in French, as if I understood! It was so embarrassing, I had to run away!'

'Col, I taught you a phrase to help with your GCSE oral, not just a chat up line for French boys!'

We go into the first tent. It's the tent of clowns. We sit on the ground, Col beside me. She's in fits of giggles. I looked at her and thought – Col and me in the tent of clowns... I think we could be happy here.

These were holiday times. Back in London school pressure was mounting. GCSEs were approaching. Old obsessions resurfaced and new ones appeared. Shopping for clothes was tortuous. If you tried on a dress that was too small you'd be distraught. You had to have exactly the same trainers as you'd had before. Of course, this wasn't always possible. You and Amanda would spend an entire day going from shop to shop. You'd come back frustrated and angry. Sometimes the search had been so absurd that it became funny.

For example, one day you went out in search for some new knickers.

'Just simple Ma, black, cotton and they're called Sloggi.'

They trawled the whole of Oxford Street all afternoon and finally found a shop that sold the brand.

'This what you had in mind madam?' smiles the sales assistant at the eager girl.

'Yes, yes but they've all got a logo on the side. I don't like it. Do you have any without the logo?'

The assistant looks at her askance. There is a pause.

'I'm afraid not madam.'

Amanda returns home with one pair and a very grumpy Col. You run into the kitchen.

'Dad, I want you to find the number for the Sloggi factory.'

'What?'

'I want you to order me a dozen pairs, black, with no logo on the side.'

'That's a ridiculous idea Col. You ask them if you must.'

I shake my head in disbelief.

'Right, I will,' you say, your green eyes flashing.

And indeed you did. You explained patiently, to the man in customer services, how there must be lots of other girls who would also like the logo taken off.

'So it would be good for everybody,' you purr into the phone. Finally you put down the receiver, smiling in triumph.

'He's going to put in my request and come back to me. He's taken our address so that he'll be able to post the knickers to me.'

A few days later a letter arrives.

Dear Ms McCulloch, thank you for your interest in our product. Unfortunately it is not economically viable for us to produce a different design for orders less than several thousand...

You rip up the letter into small pieces.

'Totally unreasonable!' you say and storm off to your room.

But sometimes your persistence paid off. Your adulation of The Rolling Stones was for the whole band and their music. But Brian Jones was the main object of your worship. You knew everything about him. How he was a talented artist and had had a place at Cheltenham School of Fine Art. You knew all about his various relationships. About how he had at least five children, two of them called Julian. You thought that was hilarious, giving two of his children the same name. You hooted with laughter when you read about it.

'Oh Brian, baby, what were you like?' you laugh.

'The two Julian Jones may not have found it quite so funny,' I point out.

'Come on Dad. It was the sixties. Even you were young then.'

You were so fascinated by Jones that you went to extraordinary lengths to find out all about him. You even tracked down Pat Andrews, the mother of Jones' third child, and started a correspondence with her. It continued for a few months. One of your favourite Stones' tracks was 'Ruby Tuesday'. You were convinced that it was originally Brian's song, and that Keith Richards reworked it. Your preoccupation with a doomed rock star seemed a bit weird but you got huge satisfaction out of researching him. One day you rushed into the kitchen.

'Mum, I've found out where Brian Jones' grave is – it's in Cheltenham. That's not far away, is it?'

It was in fact one-hundred-and-eleven miles away. But Amanda gave in and the pair of you bundled into our old Renault 11 and headed off. Sure enough, late that evening, you returned in triumph. Not only had you visited the grave, but you had got your mum to take photos to prove it. They would have pride of place in your room!

You were becoming attractive to boys and enjoyed their attention. You were happier than you'd been at any time since early childhood. You had a couple of friends. Work at school, especially in your favourite subjects, art and English, was going well. You were earning praise and being noticed.

You wrote a short story, 'The Trouble With Mr Wakefield', around this time. You wrote it for your own pleasure, not for school. It's mischievous in tone and light-hearted compared with much of your writing. I've no idea where the inspiration came from. Possibly the teacher at school who had humiliated you about dyslexia, but I don't know that. I've included extracts from Mr Wakefield. It is a surprising piece of writing for a teenage girl. Over-grown-up in some ways but frequently childish in its humour. It does however reflect an unexpected understanding of isolation:

It had become a habit of Mr. Wakefield's to let off wind
regularly when in public places. At first it was a rare
resort in times of desperation, to ease the tension in his
bowels. It became, however, a full-blown habit once he met
with bachelorhood.

Mrs Wakefield left her husband on the morning of their 30th
anniversary. She left a note by the milk. It said very little; a
list of instructions for operating the oven, the dish-washer,
and a reminder to empty the bins...

Mr Wakefield read the note, propped up by the milk that
dribbled condensation onto her carelessly scrawled words.
The kettle hissed as he let off one of, what were to be,
many lethally pungent farts. He scratched his head and
looked blankly out the window. The next door neighbour's
cat was defecating in the flower bed again...

The story goes on to reveal, in the same matter-of-fact tone, how
Mrs Wakefield has been having a clandestine affair for some years.
She has decided today to leave Mr Wakefield and go and live with
her lover. Mr Wakefield, a university lecturer, shows no outward
signs of concern, other than by letting off more wind than usual.
As the tale develops you let us know about his three daughters;
how he clearly cares for them but at a distance. How his marriage
has been dead for years. And how isolated he is, though he doesn't
seem concerned that he is. Later at work, he receives a phone call
telling him that his wife has been run over. Again, he does not
seem perturbed. He arrives at the accident scene after his badly
injured wife has been taken away. He is approached by a man he
does not know, who tries to speak to him.

'I'm... I'm.......my name is Terry. Helen and I...... We......' the words wouldn't come. Terry raised his eyes to meet those of a perplexed Mr Wakefield. At that precise moment Mr Wakefield let off wind. A great gush came out of him. His stomach rumbled in several directions. It had been silent but deadly. Terry took a few tentative steps backwards and held his nose against the smell.

'We've been lovers for three years-she was crossing the road to come and speak to you. We'd had a row, you see... Oh my God, this is all my fault. Oh my God!'

Mr Wakefield looked with disgust at the pathetic limp figure of a man, his shoulders hunched, his neck bent and cradled between his hands. He turned his back and walked towards the building.

Terry stared after him as he opened the door with discreet ease, let off another fart, and disappeared from view.[3]

---

3   From 'The Trouble With Mr Wakefield', a short story by Colette.

CHAPTER 5

Pathfinders in the Dark

The red danger signs were flashing, the sirens were coming closer, the laughter had died. I sit in front of a blank screen trying to piece together the sequences of isolation and separation that engulfed us. We were only three now. Chloe was four-hundred miles away at university, in Edinburgh. I was pleased that she was completing her education in Scotland, where I was born and grew up, but she left a gap in our family. Chloe has always been a voice of reason, a voice of calm. Amanda missed her. I missed her. But we were so pleased that she was making her own life. Mental health disorders have ruthless tentacles and we were relieved that she was now out of their reach.

You'd retreated, engulfed again in your eating restrictions and OCD big time – the demons were loose once more.

Why did you do it? Life had opened up for you. You were beautiful. As one of our friends put it, 'She's blossomed, like a little flower.' Then one day you stood in front of the mirror and everything changed.

'Oh my god what have I done? I'm fat again, fat, stupid, weak. This can't happen. I'm going to lose every ounce, every last ounce that I've gained.'

We tried to reason with you.

'Col surely you don't want to be so thin that it hurts to sit down? Surely you don't want that again? You can't live on air. You need energy to take these exams.'

It was like talking to a brick wall. You weren't deciding these actions any more than a soldier decides to duck for cover when shot at by a sniper. He doesn't think, he reacts instinctively. You were reacting to your enemy's fire. You have to be perfect other-wise they'll see through you. See you for what you are. Stupid. But that clearly wasn't what was happening. Several teachers were well aware that you wrote original and perceptive essays. One teacher read out a mock A-Level paper of yours to the class. He gave you 99%. However, that just created a huge pressure for you. You knew you couldn't live up to that. How could you achieve 99% in an actual exam?

You'd done well at GCSEs. Now A-Levels loomed. It must have been like a massive electronic road sign coming up in your brain – 'DANGER! EXAMS AHEAD'. Nothing else mattered. You had to be thin, clever, work harder and harder. You got up earlier and earlier. Set off for school at 6 am. Mum tried to stop you but you wouldn't listen. Mr Bennett, the school librarian, also got in early to prepare for the day. He told us he often saw you at the station.

'Hello Colette.'

'Oh... Hello Mr Bennett.'

They'd walk to school on opposite sides of the road. He'd unlock the school gates and in she'd go:

'Good morning, Mr Bennett.'

'Good morning, Colette.'

He said he'd never forgotten her. No other pupil would arrive for another hour and a half! He thought she was an extraordi-nary girl. He was right, you were an extraordinary girl, and you had problems.

Since Chloe's departure you started to do your homework all

over the house. You would move from room to room, to room. Every room had a problem.

'I can't work in here,' you'd scream.

'But it's the room you wanted.'

'No the ceiling slopes...the desk is too shiny...the overhead light is too low!'

No room was right. No room could be right. And so it went on.

The adolescent mental health service was called Pathfinder, The Adolescent Service. You were over sixteen now. So it was up to you whether you attended. You were to end your life resident in a clinic/care home called Pathway House. The symbolism of both names seems ironic now. What was clear to you, and eventually to us, is that they had no paths to find, let alone to tread. No real analysis. Sticking plaster for the wrong wound. Like putting a bandage on the chest of someone who in reality is dying from internal bleeding. But each visit to Pathfinders is logged as a treatment carried out. An action taken. A box ticked. A target achieved. Nobody examines the long-term outcomes. Certainly, at that time nobody addressed the fundamental question, why does this young woman keep repeating the same self-destructive patterns? The question wasn't to be answered for another seventeen years. By then far too much damage had been done.

Another appointment, another therapist, another drab waiting room. We rarely saw the same person twice. None of them had any effect on you but at least they didn't do any harm.

Unlike an incident at the child psychiatry service in 1994, when your consultant, Dr McClelland, was off sick and you were ill with gastric flu. Food, always difficult, became impossible. You started to have panic attacks daily. I contacted the hospital and a stand-in psychiatrist agreed to see you. Knowing little of your case, he dismissed your fears of food, discounted your distress and called you hysterical. You retreated into your shell.

He then proceeded to lose his temper and shout at you. He had a meltdown and completely lost control. You were frightened, shaking like a leaf, we took you out of the room. We were all very shocked.

I wrote to Dr McClelland about the incident. I still have a copy of that letter. After that incident a sequence of appointments with Dr McClelland eventually led to your referral to Woodside Adolescent Unit, mentioned earlier. They diagnosed OCD and proposed inpatient treatment. Yes it seemed to have an effect but only for the wrong reasons. You forced yourself to eat out of fear of being sent back there. It was a form of aversion therapy. They were just trying to change your behaviour without understanding why you were like you were. Without listening to you. It was never going to work. And, now as the A-Level years kicked in, it was clear it hadn't. No wonder you had little faith in doctors. We had certainly lost faith in the mental health services on offer.

Now, three years later, in Lady Margaret School's sixth form, we had to find other ways to keep you safe. We contacted the school.

'I rather look forward to our lunchtimes together Colette.'

Miss Thomas was a large, kind, Christian woman. She was head of religious studies. She was also a bit naïve. You sat alone with her, in her overheated office. She handed you your packed lunch. She had been charged with ensuring you ate your lunch each day. You unwrapped it. Miss Thomas did likewise with her much larger package. Shouted voices of high-spirited girls in the playground outside. You smile and look to a window behind Miss Thomas. She follows your eye line. You speedily remove the cheese from your sandwich and stuff it in your satchel. As Miss Thomas turns back you take a bite out of the thin bread that remains.

'I'm glad you seem to be enjoying your religious studies,' she smiles at you.

'I like the stories, Miss Thomas. The Old Testament is the best,' you reply, nibbling away.

And so you pulled the wool over poor Miss Thomas's eyes. You liked Miss Thomas. Her size reassured you. Thin women were threatening. Miss Thomas was not a threat in any way. You could manipulate her at will, just as you could the therapists at Pathfinder.

We had a good idea of what was going on but we were living in hope. Hope that if we could support you through your A-Levels, then, when the exams were over, you'd agree to have inpatient treatment for your anorexia. But in truth none of us knew what we were dealing with.

CHAPTER 6

Two As

A-Levels and Anorexia

'I have to warn you some pupils have found it a bit...er...upsetting... I mean I think it's brilliant...but we'll see what you think...' your young art teacher smiles apprehensively.

You were taking your three favourite subjects for A-Levels: Art, English and Sociology. The last two subjects were mainly judged on exam results but coursework comprised a large portion of Art A-Level. This painting would be a major part of that coursework. We knew you had been working on a self-portrait. We made our way to the art room.

Two wide empty eyes, inhabited by round black pupils, stare ahead and slightly upwards. The lashes serrated blades, spiky and black. An orange, red, white and grey mosaic colours the recognisable shape of your face. Your red mouth turned down as though anticipating the approach of something unwanted. You wear a large floppy black and grey hat and a black, buttoned top. A similarly coloured mosaic provides the background to the self-portrait (see the colour plate section). Viewed for the first time the painting is startling. The A-Level examiners also found it to be both original and skilful. You would go on to pass A-Level

Art at the top grade. The self-portrait is clearly the work of a creative, if unsettled, mind.

Your weekly appointments at Pathfinder were proving to be of no help. OCD was holding you ever tighter in its grasp. More and more rituals appeared and dominated your life. You had to click on the light five times before you went into a room. Then again five times when you left. Bedtime rituals were the worst. You had to tidy your room and rearrange the furniture to be on the same exact marks each night before you could get into bed. We could hear the sounds as you moved things around. It took up to an hour. Then everything had to be moved again before you could leave in the morning. Your meagre supper would take an age to eat. You ate no breakfast. You were disappearing before our eyes.

My dinner, lovingly prepared, adorned with all mum's special qualities. Her ability to make everything seem a present. A milky drink before bed. Hot pitta bread and marmite; (don't forget the butter!) I scorned her meals. Her presents. Her pieces of love nothing else could ever, or would ever, replace.[1]

We sought out a number of private therapists. You agreed to be taken. But once there you just played mind games. Nothing was achieved. In truth, it couldn't be. Your condition was much more complex and deep-seated, and your weight was much too low for any counsellor to deal with. But shouldn't they have known that? Since the age of twelve, when your struggles with mental health began, you saw a succession of counsellors and psychologists. Only one of them ever admitted, 'Sorry, she needs much more help than I can provide.' And that was years later when you were twenty-eight.

---

1   From one of Col's diaries.

Now you were facing the actual A-Level exams. This was the real thing. Lady Margaret School was old fashioned for the time. The pupils sat GCSE and A-Level boards that mainly assessed on exam results, not coursework. So you had a heavy schedule of papers that summer. It would have been an exhausting time for any pupil. For a girl who was so dangerously underweight that she had difficulty walking, it was a mammoth undertaking. Plus your phobias were plaguing you. Like the rustling of pages being turned, the brightness of the overhead lights and the ticking of the clock in the examination hall. It freaked you out, you couldn't concentrate. Your energy drained away as each paper was completed. Amanda had to drop you at the school gates every morning and pick you up at the end of each day. By the last exam you were near collapse but still determined to complete. Amazingly you got through and achieved two As and a B. All you could say was, 'I should have got three As.' The truth is that it was extraordinary that you completed the exams at all.

It was June, term ended, school was over. The structure you had clung to was gone. You had only one close friend, Sarah. She and two others were going on a week's package holiday to a Greek island to celebrate finishing A-Levels. They asked you to come with them. You begged us to let you go. The girls said they would all look after you, and you promised to eat. We consulted our GP. She had grave misgivings and didn't want you to go. We were in a dilemma. You would have been so upset and depressed if you'd been denied the exciting holiday. If you went it was clearly a risk and if we didn't let you go we were denying you a normal life with your friends. Catch-22.

The holiday was a disaster. You didn't eat. You drank cocktails. It was typical Greek weather – blazing June sun, scorching heat. You went to sleep by the pool and got painfully sunburnt. You paid no attention to warnings from your friends. They didn't know what to do. It was the days before mobile phones were easily available. At the airport, on your return, the girls couldn't look at us; you had lost even more weight. Your behaviour had scared them. You looked awful. With your badly sunburnt hollow cheeks, you scared us as well. We got it wrong. We should never have let you make the trip.

July was Chloe's graduation. I was away filming a TV series in northern France and couldn't get to Edinburgh. Amanda decided to go and you said you wanted to be there too. The weather played a part here as well. Only this was a typical Edinburgh summer, no scorching heat – driving rain, biting easterly blasts. It was very cold and you wouldn't wear a coat. There was a celebratory meal in the evening with Chloe and her boyfriend Teddy. You hardly ate a thing. Next morning on the platform at Waverley Station, waiting for the London train, you suddenly went very white and said you must eat. Amanda got you two sandwiches. You ripped off the packaging and gobbled down the first one while Amanda went to get you some water. By the time she got back you had swallowed the second one as well. Then you collapsed onto the ground. Amanda held you, she could barely feel your pulse; you were as cold as ice. She thought you were dying. She yelled for help.

An ambulance took you both to Edinburgh Royal Infirmary. They saw how emaciated you were and wondered why. Amanda explained you were anorexic. You were attached to various drips and were unable to speak. Through gestures, you indicated to your mum that you wanted a biro and paper. You wrote her a note on the back of an old envelope Amanda had:

Am I going to die Mum?

Amanda, shakily, wrote:

No - but you need to be in hospital.

We still have the scribbled notes.

The infirmary released you that afternoon. You spent the night at Chloe's flat, your mum beside you, afraid you might stop breathing. You both caught a train back to London the next day. I was unaware of what had happened until I came home the next week. Amanda showed me a second note you wrote a little later while in the infirmary. It reads:

> *Breathing is a little easier now. I just want to say I'm sorry. I think this needed to happen in order that I commit myself to getting better. PS - Sorry I ate your sandwiches!*

I'm sure you meant those words, even the almost comic PS. However, there was no way you could act on them; no way you could commit to getting better. You resisted treatment. Our GP was very concerned at your low weight. You had a three-week admission to the Atkinson Morley Hospital. You gained a few pounds. But you did everything you could to avoid weight gain.

You had a place at Wimbledon School of Art for a year's foundation course. A year when you could keep the doctors at bay and stay out of hospital. You couldn't, and didn't, engage at art school at all. As you wrote later:

> *My time at Wimbledon was nothing short of miserable. It was a year of frozen hands, blue lips; 'arty' parties, girls wearing wacky clothes. I couldn't blend in. My working style in art was stuck in a time warp; I couldn't seem to move on to new and varied styles of painting.*[2]

---

2   From Col's autobiography.

You made no friends. With Chloe having moved on into employment and a new flat with her boyfriend, we had downsized to a smaller house in Putney. You hated it. You wanted your old house back. Had we known then that you were autistic we would never have moved. But as it was, you lived with us for the following year in a new house that you never came to terms with. It was a difficult and unhappy time. You used to speed walk for hours by the Thames and then collapse onto your bed.

I'm running now,
or trying to.
My little knap-sack swollen
on my back, the food I've bought.
Eating like a mouse.
A few monster bites at the end
To make guiltiness grow.
But also because you're starving.
Don't the scales scream it
At you, everyday.
But creeping up, The mouse
Will panic. Put down
Its piece of well-sought cheese.
Go walking, manic speed
Down muddy lanes and
Empty landscapes.
I saw a bird, I don't
Know what. It perched
Upon a dancing branch.
It looked at me, and I
At it. He wondered at
My fleeting speed, I think,
or fancied such. I wondered

At his easy calm
Content and plump upon his branch.
Surveyor of the madness.
Lord if I could be a bird, what then?[3]

A new century was dawning, a new millennium. It was New Year's Eve 1999. A heaving crowd, millions watched the fireworks blast joyously over the Thames into the night sky. Across the world optimism briefly held universal sway. The Berlin Wall was ten years gone and the Iron Curtain. We had a new progressive government in the UK, after eighteen years of the other lot. We had peace in Northern Ireland after thirty years of the Troubles. It was a time of hope.

Our house was filled with Chloe's university friends, who stayed with us in London for the celebrations, in sleeping bags on the floor. We all went out and looked over the firework-lit water towards the newly opened Millennium Wheel, the London Eye. There was singing, hugging, kissing all around us. A wonderful youthful atmosphere. Could you and us your parents join in and feel part of this outburst of worldwide joy?

The answer of course was no. Although we were to have no understanding of your true condition for another thirteen years, we did instinctively realise there was something underlying your behaviour that hadn't been addressed. But what? Most of all we were scared that with your low weight your organs would collapse and you would die. The GP's nurse now weighed you every month. Or that was the idea. You often tried to avoid your date with the scales. Even so the records are clear. Between June and August your weight plummeted alarmingly. Your foundation course at Wimbledon finished in early summer. You were too ill

---

3   From 'Speeding', second verse, by Colette.

to take up your place at the University of East Anglia, it was too far from home. You scrambled a place at Goldsmiths in south London but you were too weak to cope. Your weight had dropped again. You were eventually admitted to Springfield University Hospital as an inpatient on 23rd November 2000 for a four-week short-stay treatment. You came home for Christmas.

By February your weight had dropped still further into the red danger level where, according to the WHO (World Health Organization), medical intervention should take place. You were at acute risk. Amanda pointed this out to the nurse practitioner, Claire, at your weekly outpatient appointment in March. And asked when you could be admitted as an inpatient.

Claire replied, 'I know her weight is very low but I have to tell you that there is no bed available for six to eight months.'

'But she's dying,' Amanda cried, 'she won't live that long.'

Col in cap aged 20

We went to see our local MP, Tony Colman, to ask for help. He was amazing. Within a week we heard there would be a bed available for you. Professor Hubert Lacey at Springfield admitted you though he never actually met you. What we didn't know was that after twelve weeks all patients had to sign an agreement that they would reach a certain BMI. At this time your BMI was far below what they were asking you to achieve. That amount of weight gain was like climbing Everest for an anorexic. You were unable to do this, so you didn't sign. At two hours' notice we were told that your psychiatrist was discharging you. You still hadn't gained any weight. They said they couldn't treat you because you were 'too ill'. I wrote to your consultant psychiatrist at Springfield about this. This is from the letter:

Dear Sir,

Re: Colette McCulloch

... You discharged Colette...at a weight...[4] well below where the WHO states a patient should be hospitalised. She did not want to leave. We were given a few hours' notice to pick her up and take her home. What if we hadn't been around? Would she have been chucked out onto the streets? Is this some tough strategy to make the anorexic face up to the reality of her illness? If so I would suggest it is an extremely brutal and dangerous one!

She was given no after care plan which, under the patient's charter, is supposed to be given to her. We also received no information about how to care for her at all. All we were given was a telephone number for Accident and Emergency for when she eventually and inevitably would collapse. You, as her consultant, made no attempt to contact us as her carers and

---

4   Specific mentions of BMI/weight have been removed in line with media advice.

parents, to explain why she was being discharged. We were just supposed to cope. To cope with a chronically ill young woman whose blood levels were dangerously out of balance and whose liver was shrinking, as later tests at the Maudsley showed.

Colette told us she was discharged because of 'behaviours'. Despite warnings she had self-harmed and she had 'restricted' her eating. Anorexics self-harm and restrict. That is how the illness manifests itself. *In other words Colette was discharged from a specialist Eating Disorders Unit because she was ill with Anorexia!* This seems inexplicable to us.

Yours sincerely

Andrew McCulloch

Despite my protest you were discharged, at this dangerously low weight, and were to receive no follow-up care. Where did that leave us? We drove to Springfield with sinking hearts and collected you and your things...

CHAPTER 7

A Life...?

Collecting Col and her things was to be a theme running through her and our lives, as we will see as her story unfolds. Some moves were difficult, some emotional, some were amusing. The final one on the day we identified her body left us numb, cold, almost beyond anger...

The reassuring PC Styles led us back through the labyrinth that is Addenbrooke's Hospital to his squad car. He drove us to Milton Park to collect her belongings, after we'd said goodbye to her in the mortuary. How do you say goodbye to a daughter that our lives had revolved around for thirty-five years? Our last contacts with her had been snatched words on mobile phones and then...she was gone forever.

We were her mother and her father. And like most parents, every instinct in our psyches was focused on protecting and nourishing both our children. It is against nature for the child to die before the parent. Over the years, we had fought to get her diagnoses, get her treatment. Now the sense of having failed her, the feeling of guilt that we'd let this happen, nearly overwhelmed us. In truth we knew it wasn't us who had let her die alone on that bleak road. Now we were on our way to pick up her things from the professionals in whose care she had been.

The small room was bare. As usual, no posters, no pictures, no ornaments – her OCD wouldn't allow that. Just a pile of small carrier bags, many still unopened. She was a shopaholic. Two shelves of jeans, skirts and dresses, mostly unworn. Books stashed in corners, Rolling Stones CDs, a Chambers dictionary, a calendar of Johnny Depp, art books, three pairs of identical trainers, copies of *Hello!* magazine, notebooks labelled 'thoughts' and her fluorescent pink Owl. So two suitcases and two boxes – a life? Is that all there is?

No of course it's not. We have her poems, we have her paintings and drawings, we have her stories and we have our memories of her. She's always with us.

'We want to say Mr and Mrs McCulloch, we are sorry for your loss...'

Two vacant-faced women stood in front of us, ill-disguised guilt in their eyes.

'Do you need any boxes for her things?'

Stonily, we took them in: the deputy manager of Milton Park and the manager of Pathway House, where Colette had lived. No sign of the actual manager of Milton Park who had admitted her. No sign of her consultant psychiatrist who was her responsible clinician, no sign of her psychologist, who had supposedly been counselling her.

'They've given up on me Mum,' she'd said on the phone. And indeed, it seemed they had. None of them had been to see her in the last six weeks of her life, not even once.

We regarded the two representatives of the private mental health provider, with cold emotion rising. I spoke for both of us and said in quiet impassive anger:

'We're not letting this pass. We will pursue you for the truth of what happened to Colette here.'

They nodded and left. Colette's belongings would be delivered to us in due course. We went out to the waiting PC Styles and his squad car. He drove us in silence back to the station. We had no idea of the processes we would be getting into. The barriers that would confront us. Just like Colette must have felt every day of her life, as she surveyed the world through her autistic eyes. As we tried to uncover the truth about her death, from the various agencies, we were to encounter denials, obfuscations, delays, mendacity and legal impediments preventing us from achieving our goal. No Yellow Brick Road lay ahead for Colette, or for us.

Part II

CHAPTER 8

Bethlem or Bedlam

I realised I was mad today
Whilst walking blindly in the rain.
The leaves made hushed whispers
As I kicked heaps across the curb.
A girl (or should I say, woman,
For that is what I am) passed me by
Un noticing. Her voice was high
With girlish giggles.
On her mobile, a painted mouth
Emitting o's of laughter.
A fountain of crinkle red hair.
And I thought, My God,
I wish that was me.
Walking in the rain with my telephone;
My connection to other lives.
It unfolded, then, in the moment
That she passed me by, with the smell
Of Tommy Girl and a gust of freshness,
Salon fresh, how lost I was.
Two women, both young, both with their lives
Before them, walking in the rain to a different tune.

How sorry I was then to think
The path I chose diverged from hers.
I watched her disappear as I charged on
Walking away from recognition.
A moment, in an otherwise blindfolded day
When I saw a woman, and a different way.[1]

17th July 2001. The Bethlem (Bethlehem) Royal Hospital is the oldest psychiatric hospital in Europe. Originally a Christian foundation, it has operated continuously, on different sites, for over 600 years. It has had a chequered and sometimes grim history. It's been inspiration for a number of horror novels and films. From the Bethlem, the nickname Bedlam (dictionary definition: 'a place of uproar, a madhouse') was coined and became part of our language. There was a horror film called *Bedlam* made in 1946 starring Boris Karloff. A campaign 'Reclaim Bedlam', started by mental health activist Peter Shaughnessy, to put right failings there, was carried out in 1997. Medical historian Roy Porter, in the campaign, called the hospital 'a symbol for man's inhumanity to man, for callousness and cruelty'.[2] It was then taken over by South London and Maudsley NHS Foundation Trust, in part as a result of that campaign.

Given its notorious history we were somewhat nervous as we drove you to the large rambling hospital for your admission. You were twenty years old. You'd been having blackouts, and you were so frail you could hardly walk. We drove into the grounds past the imposing main building and parked outside a much

---

1   'The Woman' by Colette.
2   Quoted in *Past Tense* (1999) 'Today in London's radical history: Reclaim Bedlam oppose Compulsory Treatment Orders.' Accessed on 29/07/2020 at https://pasttenseblog.wordpress.com/2016/03/15/today-in-londons-radical-history-reclaim-bedlam-oppose-compulsory-treatment-orders-1999.

more modest brick-built unit, Tyson West Two. Amanda and I walked towards it, hoping against hope that the answer to your afflictions lay in there; you followed feeling only fear I suspect. We approached reception. We later realised that it must have seemed to you that we already knew everybody there. Everyone was sympathetic and friendly. You had to sign papers saying you consented to be a voluntary patient. You seemed to accept this process but you were in such a daze, we were not sure you knew what you were doing. We headed home across London, once again leaving you in the care of strangers. Please let the treatment work this time.

The next day you sat watching the other patients. You became increasingly agitated. The penny dropped for you. You'd worked it out. You demanded that staff allow you to phone home.

'I know what you're doing Dad, it won't work,' hysteria rising in your voice. A nurse stands beside you.

'I don't understand Col. Is everything okay?'

'You know it isn't. You set this up Dad. They're all your mates, aren't they?'

'What?'

'They're not nurses and patients. I'm not stupid. They're all actors!? You've got your friends to do this! This isn't a bloody hospital!' You're shouting into the phone now.

'Colette, Colette what are you talking about? This is nonsense.'

'You can't fool me Dad. I'll get out of here and you won't ever see me again!!' The phone is slammed down.

Silence. We phone the unit. Staff reassure us, yes they have had to sedate her, but delusional behaviour like this is normal, given very low weight and the stress.

We had met Professor Janet Treasure at a conference on eating disorders some months earlier. She was approachable and friendly. She was also Professor of Psychiatry at the King's

College Hospital and the Maudsley, as well as being one of the leading world experts on anorexia. Her address to the conference was clear and extremely informative. In the wake of your sudden discharge from Springfield, we went to our GP and asked her to try and get us a second opinion from Janet Treasure's unit. The Maudsley was not in our health authority so our GP wasn't confident.

In the event, we got an appointment surprisingly quickly. Janet Treasure, in contrast to Professor Hubert Lacey at Springfield, saw you in person. She agreed that you were seriously ill and that a bed would be found as soon as possible. A week later, Janet Treasure's chief nurse, Gill Todd, called us and gave us a date for admission, which was to be in a fortnight's time.

The regime at the Bethlem was very different from Springfield. The patients all ate together. Nobody could leave the dining room until everybody had finished eating. This created peer pressure. There were pluses and minuses in this. For you it seemed to work to begin with. After your initial paranoia about Tyson West Two you started to fit in and engage. You showed interest in the other patients. You became friendly with the nurses. In the first three months your weight increased. You were still below your minimum weight, but it was the best you'd been for years. You seemed to have settled into the treatment. Our hopes rose.

We began to discuss discharge from the unit. Janet Treasure and Gill Todd thought you should move on to a halfway house; a hostel-type place where you would still have support but start to go out into the community. We visited one with you. It seemed a possibility. You were now coming home for weekends. We were having family therapy. The prognosis was good for the first time in years.

It was to prove a false dawn. Like five years earlier, when GCSEs had approached, you panicked. You became convinced that people had tricked you into eating and making you fat. All the praise they were giving you was just bullshit. You had lost control.

> So where do I turn;
> To whom can I confide when you've stripped me bare
> of all I have or hope to possess.
> Takes me back to that first dread - filled day I arrived,
> When instilled in me was the FEAR;
> That there was no way out!!
> That I had mistook a road of entrapment for escape!!
> And all I could talk about, incessantly,
> Like a crazed magpie compelled to chirp,
> Was my NEED to know I could GET OUT.
> That all doors were not barred.
> That I was as free to go as I had come.
> I was not.
> Am not.[3]

One of the dangers of inpatient treatment in eating disorder units is that patients learn 'behaviours' from each other. Anorexia is a competitive illness. When you saw someone thinner than you, it became imperative that you become that emaciated as well. Restricting eating was more difficult here but you found creative ways to do so. Local urban foxes took up residence in the grounds of your unit. No scrawny animals here, only well-fed sleek ones, feasting off the food you and your fellow patients managed to distribute! Why would they go hunting for mice and rabbits when high calorie meals appeared from on high? The

---

3   From 'Fear' by Colette.

scales can't lie is a phrase used in eating disorder units. But this is not always true. As you wrote in your 'autobiography' at the time:

I used to falsify my weight.
Even though I've stuck to same amount of water for the last two months, my weight seems to react differently every time.
Never trust water!!
Keep away from fire!!
These are the elements you can never control.

You made staff think you were doing much better than you were by using dangerous behaviours that could dilute the electrolytes in the blood and damage the brain and other organs.

Slowly, the water trickles
Painfully away during the course
of the day.
The false weight shedding its
onion layers, leaving the pale ghost
of familiar fear stalking the corridors,
Searching for shadows.
I can't believe I've trod this path again,
But it is trodden
As surely as the water drunk
In desperate, cold tiled bathrooms
Before the 'weighing-up'
No going back,
You have to keep the 'false' truth up now.[4]

---

4   'False' by Colette.

Gill Todd soon began to suspect you were up to something. She spot-weighed you one evening and found you were kilos less than it had appeared. She confronted you.

'Colette, I wasn't born yesterday. I know what you've been doing.' Gill eyeballed you. You tried to avoid her stare.

'I don't know what you're talking about Gill, I haven't been doing anything.' You open your eyes wide.

Gill Todd is one of the most dedicated nurses we've encountered in the twenty odd years we've struggled with mental health services. You had developed an adversarial relationship with her. She is someone who has seen it all and is not easily surprised. On discovering what you'd been doing she called us in.

'I know you two are actors and I'm sure you're very good at it.' Sitting in her small office she surveys us with world-weary eyes. 'But I've got to tell you that your daughter is Oscar-winning.'

She tells us your true weight. It is life threateningly below what is safe. Discharge is postponed until you prove you can maintain a safe BMI.

What I have come to learn is that all this sadness does not stem from a dissatisfaction with my weight. No, weight is not the real underlying issue for me. It's about identity and a sense of self. Sometimes I feel so non existent I have to pinch myself to remind me that I'm here.[5]

---

5   From one of Col's diaries.

Lonely as a Cloud

CHAPTER 9

A Creative Burst

A small cell-like room. Walls of peeling cream paint. No posters, no paintings, no photos. But for some clothes in the hanging cupboard it could be the cell of a Benedictine monk. All the other rooms on the ward were littered with cuddly teddies and other furry animals. Most anorexics, even the older ones, hug soft toy animals close to them for comfort, clinging to childhood. Not you. Janet Treasure remarked on how unusual your room was. She was deeply concerned at how you isolated yourself and spent so much time alone in this confined bare environment. It was put down to your OCD not allowing you to give yourself comfort. Though with benefit of hindsight the spartan room and your isolation in it are explained by your, as yet, undetected autism.

In your autobiography, written at this time, you explore your identity as you see it. You had, since a young age, always been troubled by the random nature of who you were.

I am inescapably drawn to the idea that life is made up of many different strands. That these strands form part of our past, our present and our future, and that the whole is an intricately woven fabric.

The other idea is that there are many of me, of you, of

your closest friends and family, existing at the same
time. That the life I seem to be leading now is merely one
of my many lives.
That there are many of you, living in other places and
times. Completely disparate, and yet held together by one
common bond; they are you.
But why are they you?

You went on to consider this question in relation to your circumstances in the eating disorders unit.

It's strange to think I have an identity here, but not
elsewhere. I'm a person in my own right. Not the product
of mum and dad's relationship. Not 'Andy and Amanda's
youngest daughter.'
Me; Colette Bianca McCulloch. Strange and eccentric. At
times beautiful, at others ugly in her wrath.
Colette, who is passionate about books.
Colette, who can talk for hours once she's more at ease.
And I realize, with a sharp shock, that I've made friends
during my time spent here. Some real friends [the one's I
share more in common with than the illness alone]
Friends who [I think] like me for who I am. For the dry
jokes I tell. For my company.[1]

You were right. You made friends in Tyson West Two that kept in touch with you throughout your life. One in particular, Caroline Spray, expressed what many of your fellow patients felt when she said: 'We were knocked out by Col's writing. She put into words what many of us were feeling. She was brilliant.'

---

1   From Colette's autobiography.

The thinking now is that up to 40% of anorexic girls are on the autistic spectrum.[2] Many of them would have had similar emotions. Caroline and Gemma, another friend from those days, came to your funeral all those years later.

But in the early 2000s no connection had been made between anorexia and Autistic Spectrum Disorder (ASD). The irony is that two leading world experts in the two conditions were working in the same building, metres from each other. Janet Treasure has contributed more ground-breaking research into eating disorders than almost any other psychiatrist in the last thirty years. Working close by her at the Maudsley, psychiatrist and autism researcher, Lorna Wing, was to co-initiate the Camberwell Cumulative Psychiatric Case Register. The data set out in that register established that autism was a spectrum disorder and occurred in at least one in a hundred of the population. (The accepted figure had been thought to be five in 10,000!) This meant that over 600,000 people in the UK are on the autistic spectrum. That's the population of Glasgow. Many more than had been thought. As of 2019 that figure has gone up to above 700,000.[3] At a meeting we had with leading expert Professor Will Mandy at University College London, in autumn 2019, he said that the number would be significantly higher than that if girls and women were diagnosed as efficiently as boys.

Sadly for Colette these two pioneer psychiatrists hadn't made the connection between the two conditions in 2002. Mainstream psychiatry then regarded autism as an almost exclusively male condition. It wasn't looked for in anorexic girls. Would it have made a difference had we known she was on the spectrum? We

---

2   Leake, J. (2019) 'Doctors "fail to spot autism" in thousands of girls.' *The Times*, 8 September.

3   Wing, L., Bramley, C., Hailey, A. and Wing, J. K. (1968) 'Camberwell Cumulative Psychiatric Case Register Part I: Aims and methods.' *Social Psychiatry 3*, 116–123.

think so. There were to be important decisions we all had to make later that we would have seen in a different light had we known. Fundamentally the difference is that anorexia is a mental illness, autism is a condition. Anorexia can, with timely treatment, be recovered from. Autism must be lived with, accepted and embraced, as being a part of that individual. It is not an illness like an eating disorder is. It can be very challenging but it can be extraordinarily creative. Autistic people have contributed enormously to humankind. It's not easy to live with but, if identified and acknowledged, can help give different perspectives in many areas.

Meanwhile your anorexia had to be treated, or you were going to die. When confined to your room for rest periods you would manically pace the small area, bashing disturbingly into the walls as you did so. The nurses looking after you found this deeply distressing. Other times you would pace round and round the billiard table or the art room. When allowed you would speed walk through the Bethlem grounds in all weather; working off calories, working off calories! As you write in your autobiography:

> I never used to have an exercise problem. I couldn't understand how people got so hooked on it. It always seemed so dull.
> But now I too experience the escapism of walking away. Walking away from the feelings after I've eaten, when my minds a whirl - pool of fragmented fears and images...

You wore out pairs of trainers pounding the paths and roads. You demanded replacements, but they had to be exactly the same as the old ones. This wasn't possible as makers change the designs.

'These are different, I can't wear them, I can't walk in them,' you would yell when one of us bought them for you. 'Gill told you to get them. It's all a plot to stop me walking.'

You would storm off angrily. You were being irrational it seemed to us but there were complex emotions behind these outbursts, as your poems reveal:

I miss you so much
And I wanted to tell you
But my words stuck
At the back of my throat,
And I lashed with my tongue instead.
Forgive my vindictiveness,
Because I love you so much.
You brought me a smell of home
And a feel of outside.
You were there;
I ushered you out
And you were gone.
Forgive my vindictiveness;
But don't say I'm wrong.[4]

Despite the obsession with exercise and controlling your eating, somehow the three years you spent in and out of the Bethlem were probably the most creative of your life. While there you wrote about thirty poems, several short stories, part of an autobiography and many letters. You produced some excellent drawings, you painted china, and you drew some illustrations for children's stories. How did you manage that when your focus was burning off calories and fighting Gill Todd's regime? You hated taking your medication.

---

4   'A Visit From Dad' by Colette.

Woke up this morning late again; [quarter to seven, rather than my disciplined time of six o'clock.] I'm still seething with anger. The olanzapine I'm being forced to take...is making me weak with lethargy and light headedness. I long to have the energy and stamina of before. This time yesterday I was unable to write. Imagine; never being able to keep your eyes open... I felt like I was holding up my eye - lids by a pair of precariously fitting clothes pegs. Try as I might, the pegs kept losing their hold. Closing up like some reluctant doorway.

Again, this passage is illuminating and shows some humour.

Sweet relief this morning when I saw my weight had stayed the same for three whole days!! Not only this to lift my spirits, but also that I'm feeling vaguely human again. It was too tempting to resist. Alexis [a genuinely kind woman who works night-shifts] handed me the dreaded tablet, still in it's plastic film. She seemed on the verge of asking me to 'wait' while she put things away, but I feigned deafness.
Alexis never seemed to catch up with me, as I waltzed to my room and deposited the tablet in a draw.
My heart was beating with the excitement, the sheer adrenaline of getting away with this deviant act. But there was more to my euphoria than this!! The fact that I would not be 'knocked for ten', wake - up late, and feel on the very cusp of sleep all morning long, acted as a tonic for all other concerns and anxieties.[5]

5　From Colette's autobiography.

But get going you most certainly did. Not only did you write your thoughts in poetry and prose in longhand but you would then borrow the ward computer and put the words onto it. You never liked technology but you must have somewhere realised that it was the only way to safeguard your work. It was hard graft given the limited time you had on the computer. It was a testament to how much you cared about your writing; a testament that Janet Treasure and Gill Todd picked up on.

You had always said that you wanted to study English at university and become a writer. You'd gained a place on the Creative Writing course at the University of East Anglia. You had been too ill to take it up. Other universities had also accepted you. Now in 2002 you were offered a place at King's College London to study English Literature. You told Janet and the team that was your goal. You would get better, you would put on the necessary weight, you would do anything in order to take up that place. It was the incentive you needed to banish your anorexic demons you declared.

> I'm desperate to get out of here, but if I'm honest I'm quite scared as well. 'Tyson West Poo' has been a feature in my life for the last two years and I've forgotten what real living is.[6]

Janet Treasure and Gill Todd were sceptical. Your BMI was still far too low. You needed to gain weight. As spring turned to summer, there was still little sign of you reaching a safe target. Despite that you argued persuasively that going to university was the one ambition you had. If the team stood in your way

---

6   From one of Col's diaries.

it would be very damaging to you. You began to feel more and more trapped.

> There is nothing save fear
> In this furnace brain of mine.
> Nothing but frenzy
> In this state of mine.
> What will they do to me,
> How can I know
> When I'm lost and I'm sinking
> And I've nowhere to go?[7]

By September, not long after you wrote that poem, Janet Treasure called us all in. She said that she had decided to give you a chance. Since King's College was in London you would be reasonably safe. We, your parents, would be close by to keep an eye on things. The Bethlem would keep your bed available in case things went wrong. So you could take up your place at King's College for your Freshers' Week. Now you were no longer lost and sinking with nowhere to go. You were off to university...

---

7   From 'Sinking' by Colette.

CHAPTER 10

Cry Freedom

From Colette's handwritten diary dated 2002 and titled *This is a Book about Me.*

> I was being given the chance to live outside and attend university to study English Lit, at King's College, London. I was genuinely excited.

We were concerned that you would not be able to cope with the stress of a degree course. However, we agreed that having the opportunity to study your beloved English Literature might be the motivation for you to finally confront your demons. You were to live in halls for the first year. We drove you to the residence on the South Bank of the Thames with your books, clothes and other possessions. The size and the anonymity of the place worried us. We said that you could always stay with us if you felt lonely. Putney was only a short train journey away after all. But you were determined to be part of uni life. Living with us oldies would cramp your style. So once again we drove away leaving you in a strange place on your own. However, a university degree in English was your dream. You were twenty-one years old and that dream was beckoning.

But it was too easy. Ten years and then eating and off to university... I couldn't stop walking, so how could I study? I wandered round and round Covent Garden. Like the billiard table (on the ward). I was getting tighter & harder & smaller & more impenetrable. A little bullet waiting to be triggered.

You wrote that some weeks later. At the time it soon became apparent that you were missing many seminars and lectures. We would ask you how they went. You gave us vague and unconvincing answers. When we talked to you at the end of each day, we realised that you had made no connection with other students. You didn't know anything about them. At the Bethlem you used to comment on what Caroline or Gemma might be up to. At King's College you didn't even know any of your fellow students' names.

I cannot always decide whether what's happening is imagined or otherwise. My eye-sight doesn't help... I am never able to decipher facial expressions or subtle allusions to this or that. It makes me even more paranoid that I'm acting out of context.[1]

Your eyesight was very similar to mine. You were short-sighted but otherwise you had no problems. It is true that you often didn't read people's real feelings. I don't think that was to do with eyesight but more to do with the way you interpreted people. You would misread their true intentions by taking literally what they said rather than understanding their body language and facial expressions. Like if a man said, 'Colette you have beautiful green eyes,' you thought they were a good person. This despite the fact they were only really eyeing up your purse to see if they could get

---

1   From Colette's autobiography.

some money off you. And like when you were younger and we all
went to the cinema as a family. We'd come out when it finished and
discuss the film. It was as though Chloe, Amanda and I had seen
one film and you had seen a completely different one. Your inter-
pretation of *Thelma & Louise* was nothing like ours. We would look
at you in amazement as you expounded your version of the story.

'Wow Col your imagination is something else!' Chloe laughed.

Your offbeat understanding of events and emotions was to
lead to you having original and creative insights. But it was also
to lead to confusion and a lack of understanding from those
around you – including us your parents.

After three weeks you came to the same conclusion that we
had about university. You wrote in your autobiography about
the decision:

> I tried university as an incentive to change my life, the way
> I think. An incentive to get and stay well. But I realised,
> after three pathetic weeks, I wasn't ready...

Janet Treasure had kept your bed for you. You had lost more
weight in your time at King's College. Everyone on the team
agreed that you could not be expected to make any rational
choices when you were so severely underweight. You certainly
could not be expected to study for a university degree. We were
in complete agreement with your readmission to hospital.

Crises occur in families and life goes on. Your granny, my
mum, was a strong woman, she had lived a full if difficult life.
She had gone through the war on her own looking after my older
brother. My father was a pilot who was frequently stationed in
the Far and Near East. When he was demobbed after the war they
bought a small dairy farm in Ayrshire. It was hard work and they
were always in debt. But she came through and was an important

presence in your, and Chloe's, lives. The same October you gave up King's College, she, at eighty-nine years old, contracted pneumonia and died quite quickly. Hers was a life to celebrate, not mourn. Given your state of health your reaction was surprising and in a way heartening:

I'll always recollect your hands,
Their character and form.
The way you pored the tea at five,
And the rhythm of the Grandfather clock
That always stood, resolute and proud;
Respectful that it's Tea -Time.
The sound of clinking china,
A cup and saucer. Slice of currant cake,
So comforting to remember,
Devastating to lose.
And on cold mornings
We'd wake you up with excited dogs and leads;
The first of many walks.
Wellingtons and mackintoshes,
Armed with matching umbrellas
We were careered by eager mongrels
Along the hills framed by your window.;
Magical to remember the golden afternoons
Spent languidly in deck chairs,
The weekend papers turning in the breeze
And all your books piled high.
The garden that went up and up,
The stone steps and Hyacinths and clematis
And you dizzying my child-like wonder
With all this easy mustered magic.
The way you made your world:

My place in it,
But, oh, how separate do I see myself
Now, when you are gone,
The papers yellowed and afternoon
Is night.[2]

You were genuinely upset by her death. Despite being able to write an appreciation like that you were unable to make rational decisions about your own life.

On 13th November a ward round took place at the Bethlem. Dr Webster was not a favourite of yours. A burly male psychiatrist in his forties, he, in the eyes of the almost exclusively female patients, played bad cop to Janet Treasure's good cop. He was running this meeting. I quote below an extract from a report made by the registrar.

> At the Ward round on 13th November taken by Dr Peter Webster, Miss McCulloch was adamant that she was only willing to gain weight to [a still dangerously low BMI]... It was, therefore, proposed that she would be assessed for treatment under a section of the Mental Health Act. Dr Webster felt that she lacked capacity to acknowledge the significance of her weight... Approximately one hour after this Miss McCulloch was found face down, unconscious [having self-harmed].

It is relevant that Dr Webster comments that you 'lacked capacity'. This was an opinion that was to recur. In the years to follow your mental health would deteriorate. A number of experts noted that you lacked capacity. However, certain mental health professionals at Milton Park and Bedford Adult Mental Health

---

2   'Gran' by Colette, 2002.

Professional (AMHP) service were unwilling to acknowledge this. Back at the Bethlem, you wrote about the meeting with Dr Webster and your reaction to it in graphic terms.

I walk out when it's over, down the dark echoing corridor.
I know what to do.
I climb in to the bath; the void.
The bath water turns orange. I slide. I don't feel weak; only calm.
The little threads of blood...playing games between my toes. A slow ebbing away and beyond the reach of noise. I hold my breath under water. Count. Stop counting. A flood in my windpipe. Swallowing and spluttering. I cannot breath - Lauren is holding my head on the side of the bath, my ear pressed on the cold of the bath edge.

Charcoal self-portrait sketch

You were now to spend the next seven months sectioned under the Mental Health Act. You said you hated being confined and watched all the time. You complied though. You gained weight. You didn't reach their target, but your BMI, while still low, was the safest it had been for years, and you maintained it. It was commonly thought that if a patient sustained a healthy BMI for some time, the illness would recede. However, despite your physical progress, your mindset hadn't changed. By June 2003 the team thought it was time you moved on, into supported living, a halfway house. They felt there was no more they could do for you. The idea being you would, with help, gradually adjust to life outside. You didn't like the one that the Bethlem recommended. We found an alternative up in Norwich. After an interview it was agreed you would go there for an assessment with a view to long-term care. But in your heart, you were never convinced by the placement. You wanted out altogether. You yearned for freedom. Freedom from what, or for what, I don't think you knew. Other than freedom from people controlling what you did.

The treatment you received from Janet Treasure and her team at the Bethlem was second to none. They saved your life. You saw expert psychiatrists, psychologists, occupational therapists, clinical nurse leader, etc. They were a dedicated team who genuinely cared about their patients. They were devastated if a patient died. At least two staff members made it to your funeral to pay their respects, thirteen years after you were discharged.

So what went wrong? Why wasn't there a positive outcome for you? I would suggest the clues are all around. While writing this we have gone through many papers from that time. Your own autobiography provides many insights into what we only much later came to know as your autism. A phrase you mention about your time at King's College University rings out now when I read it:

> I couldn't comprehend the normality of those around me. What made them tick and how?... I am never able to decipher facial expressions or subtle allusions to this or that.

And interestingly a summary written for you by a trainee clinical psychologist, who worked with you for many months, alludes to your true condition, without identifying it. It was written just before you started at King's College. This is an extract from it:

> You described to me a feeling of needing to escape from 'The Void' which we decided is a feeling of emptiness and nothingness where you would feel nothing but would be aware of this. This frightens you a lot. You have an image of yourself as a statue made of all the phobias and obsessions that you seem to use to keep yourself feeling 'real'. If these were taken away then your image of yourself changes to a puddle of jelly on the ground; you collapse. All of your worries, therefore, seem to act as a way of not facing the void, of making sure that it can't 'get' you. It is hard for other people to understand this, but it means that worrying and obsessing about things are better than the possibility of feeling nothing...

Janet Treasure said early on in your admission that your isolation was what puzzled her most, and, again, I agreed. But the connection wasn't made. Looking back, it seems clear to me that the isolation was a product of your, as yet undiagnosed, autism.

CHAPTER 11

The Umbilical Cord

3rd October 2003. Mixed emotions in the car as we drove back down the M11 from Norwich. I was at the wheel, Amanda beside me. You were in the back. The classic picture of a child being taken home by her parents - only you weren't a child and hadn't been for some years. Amanda and I were deeply depressed; we knew you'd made a very bad decision. You'd been in and out of hospital for years - none of them had worked. You needed a different approach, a different environment. Newmarket House Clinic is a large detached house in Norwich, with a garden and only twelve patients. We'd fought for six months to get you the NHS funding for a place there. The clinic believed in a calm, holistic approach so that the body and the mind became less stressed, and recovered. The food was healthy and organic. They were committed to supporting you in getting voluntary work in the town and learning how to cook for yourself. They weighed patients, but in order to take the obsession out of the whole business, kilos weren't discussed. You absolutely freaked at not being told your weight. You'd lost control. That couldn't be allowed to happen.

'Bunch of stuck up cows. Weighing me but not telling me

what it was. "Nah, nah, nah nah nah, you're not allowed to know Colette!"'

'You didn't give it chance, Col. You were only there for a month.'

'"And no running along the corridors, Colette!" Control freaks!' you mocked. 'Face it Dad, I was never going to get better in that dump.'

Amanda sighs, 'Col, you know the only other option at the moment is a mixed psychiatric ward. Do you really want that?'

'I don't have to go anywhere. Just let me be. I'll get better at home.'

'Col, how many times have you said that? If you don't eat, if you don't stop walking, we can't keep you safe.' I reply.

We passed a motorway sign saying it was fifty miles to London. We had run out of arguments. We were all silent. You were nearly twenty-three. You were unable to live on your own or hold down a job. You had tried university. You had been unable to cope and nearly collapsed. We'd tried NHS therapists, private therapists, two NHS eating disorder units and a private clinic. None of them had got through to you. You appeared to be unreachable. What the hell do we do now?

> You're a retrogression,
> I think in retrospect.
> A hole without a meaning,
> A post-box with nothing to put in.
> You sit and you stand
> And you walk and you talk.
> You dilly and you dally
> And you smile all aquiver
> With a never ending fear.
> You're a box of dislocated nerves,

You're a catastrophic mixture
From something in the lab.
An experiment of Gods,
A Jesus for the devil.
A pen without the ink,
A life without the soul.
I had a soul but,
How shall I put it?
I lost it, if you really
Must know. When
I was six, and it decided
to go.[1]

There was a pervasive undercurrent of thinking in those days, and still is to some extent, that mental illnesses like anorexia were the fault of bad parenting. In particular, these accusations were made against mothers of ill children. I have to make two aspects around this issue very clear. Firstly, we reject this criticism on behalf of the many loving parents we have met, who have struggled to support children with a variety of mental health conditions. Secondly, at the Maudsley, Janet Treasure and her regime totally dismissed any theories like that. Her entire team was always very supportive. Nevertheless, mother blame was, and still is, common. You yourself commented on your deep attachment to your mum in your journal, written some years earlier while in the Bethlem:

Mum loved me and looked after me...
I was always too attached to my mother. It was not that
I was clingy, for this I was not. More to the point, I was

_____

1   'When I was Six' by Colette.

forever trying to keep her in sight... She was always small and sharp and sparkly, flitting this way and that like a butterfly who will not keep still.

Cartoon – 'Mother's Day'

I wanted her all to myself... I wanted mum to be as watchful of me as I was of her.

However, the Springfield medics at this time were rather more sceptical about family attachments. This is a quote from a letter written to us by one of the doctors:

I did not tell you to stop protecting Colette and that she should not be living with you... I said that you might be prolonging her anorectic wish to remain at a lower weight, by keeping her propped up...

The theory is that, in part, eating disorders were a way of not growing up; not becoming a woman. By maintaining a very low weight, young women don't menstruate and remain childlike. Parents can contribute to this by continuing to treat their daughters as though they were twelve years old, when in fact they may be twenty or thirty. The umbilical cord must be cut. A distance should be put between child and parent if the child is to grow into an adult. We now realise this is a simplistic explanation of a complex condition. As Professor Will Mandy explained to us at our meeting, 'It is now clear that up to 40% of anorexics are on the autistic spectrum. And autistic people tend to benefit from close support, not tough-love distancing.' He went on to explain that the National Autistic Society now states that 'normal' treatment for anorexia doesn't work for anorexics on the spectrum. It often does more harm than good.

However, it was to be another ten years before you were to be diagnosed with autism. You were back living with us in London and we did just seem to be supporting your illness. You went on long power walks every day. We would see you steaming along the Thames towpath near our home. You didn't see us, your eyes glazed with purpose, staring myopically ahead as you charged on. As you wrote at the time:

Swaying. Coming to
And falling
Narrow exits never
Thought of getting through.
Faces swimming in the Dark.
Beautiful, to listen to this
Silence, deep within, while all
outside there's noise
And bustle.

But I am
Woven in a Web of
Thermal jumpers and
Layers of coat.
A little pea-head in a
Swamp of melted Liquorice
Speeding through the
Human traffic
Lights, lights everywhere
Fermenting in my mind.[2]

Autumn turned to winter; you walked and walked and walked. We had to find something constructive for you to do. Something to help you engage with the world. We enrolled you into pottery classes at the local art college. You weren't strong enough to work the clay on the wheel. We found a Creative Writing course for you at Roehampton. You went for a few weeks but didn't really like it. And every day you walked, and walked and walked.

Your mental health treatment had reverted from the Maudsley back to Springfield. Your consultant there was becoming more and more concerned about your walking and your weight loss. On 12th January 2004 she insisted you were admitted for a short stay to regain weight and try to break your addiction to exercise. You had been in Springfield only three years earlier for your first admission to an eating disorder unit. You describe that stay in the acute care ward:

I lay in that wobbly bed (I imagined myself stretched out on an enormous jelly) and regretted all those opportunities I'd had on the Ward to add back the foods I'd cut out.

---

2 From 'Speeding', first half, by Colette.

But I was, deep down, relieved that I no longer had to fight 'the Voice'. I no longer had to fight the war between myself and 'it'.

I read profusely. I devoured book after book, as though this were my substitute to starvation; it fed a part of me that needed feeding other than my physical self.

When I read 'A Tale of Two Cities', 'To Kill A Mocking Bird', 'Girl with Green Eyes', 'Wuthering Heights, I was transported to another place; another time. I was able to become someone else, briefly, before the meals arrived to upset my sense of balance.[3]

You devoured some great literature during that admission but your mindset remained stuck. This 'short stay', three years after your first admission to Springfield, turned out to be twelve weeks. They tried giving you clomipramine and other drugs with no success. You were discharged at roughly the same state as when you'd been admitted. 'The drugs don't work anymore,' they never did. Nor did the treatment. Of course it didn't work, they weren't dealing with the right condition. Now you were home with us in Putney once more, pounding the Thames footpath.

Like a never ending wheel that keeps spinning my mind running marathons. Across ditches, between fences. The assault course of the senses. There's a light, but it keeps fading. There's a hope (but it doesn't last) that I'll get through this somehow.[4]

---

3   From Colette's autobiography.
4   From Col's diary.

We were desperate. We decided we must try a radical step. In rural France there is a tradition of healers, called *Guérisseurs*, who have the ability to take the heat out of an illness, mental or physical, by laying on of hands. We had been told of one highly respected *Guérisseur* by the name of Gérard. He lived near our cottage in the Tarn in south-west France. We decided to take you down there for an extended stay. To get you away from all the London-centric pressures; all the ultra-skinny models and female celebs, vying for media coverage in *Hello!* magazine. The hope was that Gérard might take the heat out of your anxiety in the calm rural environment.

I'm normally sceptical about alternative healing. I can only say that on meeting Gérard his gentleness and empathy dissolved any doubts. He accepted no money. 'My gift is handed down to me, recompense is in the healing.' There was another reason for our trip to the Tarn. April and May are often beautiful months there. The countryside bursts into life. The trees are quickly blanketed in green. Daffodils and roses flourish before your eyes. And there were memories down there of sun-drenched optimistic summers past. Maybe somewhere they might rekindle emotions; good times you shared with Dominic and friends eight years earlier? Memories you wrote of while in the Bethlem:

And I was a flitting like a butterfly. I would never settle. I was beautiful, too... His best friend liked me, and I liked him because of Dominic. Because every connection to Dominic was potential access to him... I flirted... But I was playing a part... I was metamorphosing in to the girl of my dreams. Pink plimsolls, blonde hair... I was invincible. It was impossible not to love me!...
It was all a dream, to imagine these nights bleeding in to days. For the world is a different place at night. When the

sun's packed away; the stars sent out in troops, and the
canopy of darkness like a shroud thrown over all, we inhabit
a new dimension. Separate to that of day.
At night Colette is different.[5]

Maybe revisiting the scene could help you throw off the shackles
of your illness? It was another dream, but if nothing else we
would have a couple of months in a decent warm climate, eating nutritious local food. Meanwhile you walked and walked,
as before. Would you get lost? A little network of local friends
sprang up. They knew you; Jean-Claude, Sally, Michelle, Puck
and Lorraine. You'd leave the house in the morning. Hours would
pass. The phone would ring. 'Col's just passed us near the café. I
think she's heading in your direction.' There was a rural safety
net. It was reassuring and you never did get lost.

Of course our two months in the Tarn didn't have the magical
effect we were seeking. You came with us to see Gérard but never
engaged. All you saw was a rather weird old man. At the end
of May we packed up the car, and the three of us headed the
seven-hundred miles back to London. The same configuration
once again; us in the front, taking turns to drive, you childlike
in the back.

---

5   From Colette's autobiography.

CHAPTER 12

Birkbeck

Vibrant Learning

Back in London life resumed the same routine of power walking and food restriction. Your weight had been hovering at a dangerously low point since our return from France. By September your consultant decided something had to be done. You were admitted to a different ward in Springfield once again. You were to be kept under closer observation. Your eating was carefully monitored, your walking was to be curtailed. This 'short stay' ended up lasting eight months. You were alive but little psychological progress had been made.

> But, ten years on,
> It's different now.
> Worse, because I haven't got the adrenaline
> I had from not eating. The sense
> of power and control...
> Because it's different now
> To how it used to be.
> I cannot seem to change my thoughts
> And find myself gravitating always.

Always in one direction.
It's different now because I know
And feel the waste of it.
I don't know how
Or if I want to change.[1]

Our lives were equally fettered. For the last ten years, most of our family life had revolved around trying to find the right treatment for you. Anorexia has the highest mortality rate of any mental health disorder.[2] The statistics are alarming. Keeping you alive had been the priority. However, as we had been told, we were only supporting the illness, not curing it. Amanda and I came to a critical decision. We discussed it with Chloe and she agreed with us. We must make you realise that we had our own lives and we intended to live them. Hopefully this would edge you towards changing the course you were currently following.

We were in our early sixties by this time. We felt we needed a project to take us into our retirement. We planned to sell our cottage in the Tarn. Then we would buy another rundown stone building and renovate it. For the moment we would keep a place in London. We told you of our plans. Showed you photos of semi-ruined houses we potentially might buy. We said that you and Chloe could come and stay, whenever you wanted and for as long as you wanted. We explained it would be our retirement project. You wrote letters to us about it from Springfield. Below are extracts from your handwritten letters:

---

1   'It's Different Now' by Colette.
2   Beat (n.d.) *About Us*. Accessed on 02/07/2020 at www.beateatingdisorders.org.uk.

Dear Mum and Dad,

... After I spoke to mum (on the phone) about the
possibility of the house you've both discovered in
France, I felt so elated! It's so exciting!!
...I really mean it about the house. It sounds brilliant;
a project for us all!... As mum said on the phone; 'There's
so much out there - Grab it! Grab it with both hands...
And so I will, mum & dad. Tentatively, I will untie the
mask that has covered my face for so long. I will allow
myself to see beyond the peripheries of my enclosed,
insular existence.

Much love, Col X

On reflection, letters like that may have been you saying what
you thought we wanted to hear. A typical autistic response, we
have since learned. Sadly I think our plans just increased your
anxiety. A letter written after a weekend visit home to us betrays
your feelings more accurately:

Sorry I wasn't more animated/sociable when we had
Cheryl, Carole, Chloe and Teddy round to supper. I still
find it quite difficult to inter-act with people, particularly
in larger groups and gatherings...
People have commented on how isolated I make
myself on the ward...as dad said to me on the phone: I
find it very hard to just 'be'.
Thanks for bringing the shampoo.

Much love Col X

You were still self-harming on the ward. You disturbed the nurses with your manic exercise and scoring your scalp with your nails. Your poem 'Be To Be' describes your anxieties. This is an extract:

> So when you're lost
> Let your mind take sanctuary
> In something you can
> Believe, and be patient.
> The road is rocky
> And we are all scared and
> Running,
> But we're together.
> Reality is within you.
> Shape it right, and try
> To just be.[3]

17th May 2005 you were finally discharged from Springfield. For all your optimism, 'To just be' was an unattainable Holy Grail for you. You could write about it. You could imagine and describe it. But live it...?

So yet again, it was the three of us. Six years since you left school. Six years in and out of clinics and hospitals. Six years of inpatient care, outpatient appointments, psychology and therapy sessions. However, your weight was still dangerously low and your mind as stuck as ever. When you left Springfield this time you were given a social worker. Patrick Bull was a diligent guy in his early forties. He established an easy rapport with you. We worked with Patrick on finding projects for you to be involved with. You said you liked old people. We found a lunch club for

---

3   From 'Be To Be' by Colette.

the elderly. You went and assisted. The old people liked you. But you often became bored and went walking. You wanted to help kids who were dyslexic. We found a local primary school. It took you on as a voluntary helper, working one to one with seven-year-olds. Soon you were missing sessions. And still you walked and walked.

> And I don't know what it is, to let go. Let go the rope around my neck. To unfasten the chains around my wrists. So I dream. I dream, and tell stories, and hope that one day these wild fantasies spring to life.[4]

But as we moved into the spring of 2006 you were beginning to eat better or at least more. You would get so hungry that you'd binge eat; then the guilt. Little by little, your bone-protruding shoulders looked less frightening. Your stick-like arms fleshed out slightly. Your lollipop face came into proportion. However, your moods became if anything more fractious. You would frequently scream at us in fury for moving an object or leaving food on a table. Rows would erupt out of nothing. In truth you were terribly lonely. All your old school friends had moved on and were with boyfriends and had jobs by now. Sometimes you would storm off out of the house, into the night, declaring you were going to run away to anywhere. Anywhere would be better than being here, with us. One night mum found you, sitting on your own, in a rough old pub off the High Street.

'Col, what are you doing here?'

'I thought I might find my Prince Charming, Mum.'

'Oh Col, you won't find "Prince Charming" in a place like this.'

---

4   From Col's autobiography.

Amanda put her arms round you and led you home. It was indeed your 'wild fantasies' that filled your mind.

> It is my dreams, the stories told in my head that feel more true. No matter what actually takes place. My dreams dictate my reality.[5]

Other times, you would go missing in the middle of the night. We'd find your empty room. I would spend hours, torch in hand, combing the riverbank, fearing what I might find. Then you would phone us from an A&E nearby, asking us to fetch you home.

I suppose it was your hormones raging, brought on by your starting to eat again. You were now 25 years old and it was as though you were going through a very late puberty. Teenage years can often be difficult. A teenager in her mid-twenties was something else altogether. Patrick Bull agreed that your living with us was unhealthy. You must establish yourself as an adult away from us. It was a vital part of your recovery to live away from your parents.

> And what now?
> Apparently you are supposed to 'grow up' in to a thing we call an 'adult'.
> You are supposed to become your own person;
> independent of your parents... You are supposed to let go of the past, however precious...
> You are supposed to do your bit in the world...
> You are supposed to cope for the time you wander

---

5   From one of Col's diaries.

this earth; for that is all there is and all you will ever
know. Beyond this there is nothing.
Nothing. Why does nothing scare me so?[6]

You wrote that a couple of years earlier. It was as if anticipating
what the future held. Patrick Bull recommended very strongly
that Social Services find you a flat, and we agreed with him.

This was far from easy, however. After a couple months of
waiting, Social Services turned Patrick Bull's request down.
Once again there seemed to be no way forward. So once again
we approached our local MP. Tony Colman, who had helped you
last time, had lost his seat. Justine Greening was the new MP. We
wrote to her explaining your predicament and mental health
history. We saw her in her surgery. She quickly grasped the situation. She put our case to social housing but even then it took
a further four months for accommodation to be found for you.
Without Justine Greening's persistence this would never have
happened. Finally, on 24th June 2006 you moved into a small
one-bedroom flat, in your Wandsworth flat. It was close by. You
were excited. A future beckoned.

There was support for you from Social Services. They helped
you organise rent payments, electricity and phone. You had a
mobile phone for the first time. Patrick Bull visited you frequently to begin with. Learning how to manage living from day to day
took up much of your time at first. He set up a team who would
help you with various practicalities like direct debits, weekly
budgeting, etc. You still wanted to go to university. It was now
over seven years since your A-Levels. After that time, universities
required that you take an access course before being accepted.

---

6   From one of Col's diaries.

We helped you enrol at Birkbeck College to take a course leading to a degree in English Literature.

'Student Reading'

Birkbeck holds evening courses for part-time students. Your access course required you to travel across London to Blooms-bury two evenings a week. We were nervous about you managing this. In the event you did. As the course developed you got more and more out of it. It helped that your tutor really liked your work. You made some contact with other students. At the end of the course you passed with a distinction.

However, the course didn't occupy all your days or evenings. Your eating was still chaotic, but you were coping and reaching a safer and healthier weight. But you were lonely, especially at weekends. You began to discover clubs, alcohol and men. You got into some scrapes but you soon found a regular boyfriend, which calmed things down.

You were besotted with Inis. You said he was lovely. You explained how his English wasn't very good and he made you laugh at his mistakes. We asked where he came from. You weren't sure. Geography and knowledge of countries were never your strong point.

'What's it matter? Algeria, think he said. Yes, Algeria,' you confidently told us.

'Oh right, he speaks French then?' asked Amanda.

'Don't know. But he asked me to pick up his clothes and iron his shirts when I stayed at his. Apparently Muslim men expect their women to do that.'

'I don't suppose you did,' Amanda laughed.

'Course not. But he is beautiful Ma.' You produced a small photo-booth photograph. He was certainly good looking, with dark hair but what seemed to us a very European face.

'Are you sure he's from Algeria Col? He doesn't look African,' I probe.

'Yes I'm sure, near Greece he said.'

'Near Greece? Do you think he said Albania?' I tentatively suggest.

'Maybe. Whatever, who cares? I'm going to wear my new top when I see him this evening Mum.'

We never did meet Inis. He did turn out to be Albanian and determined not to ever go back there. You told us he asked you to marry him. You liked the idea. We advised caution. You didn't listen. Luckily you talked about it to a French girl who was waxing your legs at a beauty salon, a few days later. She told you: 'Colette, no, no don't marry. I have a friend who met a man like this. He just wanted a passport. Get to know him better first.'

Luckily you listened to her. In the end you decided you wanted to study for a degree, more than you wanted a life picking up Inis's clothes! You had gained a place at the University of Sussex, near Brighton, to study English Literature. You told us you would try and continue the relationship with him while at uni. A few weeks later you went to London to visit him. Inis already had a blonde, blue-eyed English girl in tow, whom he later married.

I think
What I loved about him most
Was his natural happiness.
The smile
That played upon his face
Was the opposite of mine.
Mine to be the one
Induced by drink
And false make up
And words I dread to hear, for now
All I feel for him
Is pure, unadulterated desire.
But it is different now.
The boy with dark brown eyes
Looks in to blue.
They are not mine,
And I do fear they are the ones he always wanted.
Dark boy meets light girl.
Is that not the case?
And was I not always somewhat
Much too dark?
I miss you.
I miss laughing with you
At absurdities
And unequivocal misunderstandings
Because your English was so dreadful
And my blaspheming similarly so.
And I miss looking at you in repose.
And touching your upper arm

And travelling the line of your spine;
The smooth depth of your oliveness.
I miss you so much that the
Irony of your words hits me now
When I remember you saying
'Never forget me.'
How strange
For it would seem, my love,
You've done enough forgetting for both of us.[7]

You weren't heartbroken but you were understandably hurt. However, you were on your way to fulfil your dreams. You had reacquainted yourself with academia at Birkbeck. You had learned about living in the real world in your East Hill flat. You had had your first full relationship with a man. You had been able to move on from that and to gain a place at university, as a mature student. For the first time in years, Amanda and I felt optimistic about the future...

---

7 'What I Loved' – Colette's first poem at university.

CHAPTER 13

The Undergraduate

It's nose to tail. The A27 cuts a swathe of tarmac and concrete through the green of the East Sussex countryside. Suddenly the 'plate-glass', 1960s structures of the University of Sussex appear on our left. We just manage to make it across to the slip road and seek out your new home. Stanmer Court Flats have only just been built, the scaffolding has barely been removed. You are among the first students to move in. It's a flat for four mature students. You are 26 years old now. You're to share with a woman taking her second degree, studying medicine this time, and two male students in their mid-twenties. You have a bedroom with an en-suite shower and loo. You're to share the kitchen and sitting area.

We move your stuff into your room. We all say hello to two of your flatmates. They seem friendly. Then the moment comes for us to say goodbye. Once again your parents are leaving you on your own in a strange place. Only this time it is where you want to be, doing what you want to do. We all three felt positive if nervous. This is the opportunity you'd been striving for through your time at school, in hospital and at Birkbeck, where you had studied with such distinction.

Perhaps we should have taken more note of what you had

written during those years. Stories like the one inspired by your previous attempt at studying for a degree. 'The Incomplete', in many ways, describes the challenges of your autism, without you even being aware of what autism is...

Travelling alone in the dark, Helen looked around her to seek some comfort in the faces of those who sat, hunched against the cold. Some were engrossed in books, others just staring, blank eyed, out towards the passing scenery.

Up until now she hadn't been aware of her surroundings, or the people with whom she shared the carriage. Helen had been lost in her own thoughts. At these moments, everything outside of herself recedes in to a clear blue, and the conversations begin in her head. The constant worrying. The need to put her world in order; to draw some lines through which to channel her energy. She felt shapeless; bottomless. Without the means of self-containment. She felt utterly alone, until she saw his face.

Unlike the other passengers, he was not reading or gazing at the dancing trees and hedgerows that stretched past them. He was looking at her.

Every now and then his eyes would reach for her from the back of the carriage. They were furtive glances, stolen but prized. For Helen, they were like beams of light in an otherwise pitch-black world.

Helen had felt strange all day. After meeting up for a drink and a chat with an old school friend, she felt even stranger. She couldn't conceive herself to be the same person that trod alongside Jane Ashwood all those years ago, on their way to dreaded school.

Jane seemed much the same; all red-bow lip-stick and

bubbly laughter. Chunky, in a soft way, with creamy skin like a baby's. Very popular with the boys.

Snippets of their conversation come back to her whilst on the train; 'You look so cold, Helen. Where've you been?'

It was hardly the warmest welcome she'd received from a friend she hadn't seen in over seven years.

If the ugly, brutal truth be known, Helen was contemplating suicide again. She had a tendency to do this when her world became out of focus. It was like an inevitable transition from one thought to the next. A sequence of images. Her mum's old lampshade. Her childhood home, and the way the carpet on the stairs tickled her feet when shoeless.

Then the tiles by the bath. Lots of running water and a flooding of memory. She knew it was melodramatic... She knew that if she told about these thoughts they'd think her the self-obsessed type who found the illusion of death romantic. Poetic. Sylvia Plath. Ophelia

Then his face, his eyes like two sharp pebbles, blinking in the electric light.

Now she was thinking about the man on the train, looking at her. Now she was thinking; It's all right. I'm attractive. We'll fall in love and get married. My life will be worth mentioning. I'll be part of something bigger than myself. Perhaps I'll even have babies, like other women do.

She approaches him. She does not hesitate. She sits down in the seat opposite and smiles. 'Hello. My names Helen. Sorry to disturb you, but I couldn't help noticing you.'

'Oh, hello. Yes, I saw you too. You looked slightly lost.

'Yes, well no, actually. I was just a bit down. I met up with an old school friend this evening and she's achieved so much. It makes me feel like a bit of a failure. Like, I've done nothing with my life. Honestly, I haven't. If you were to ask me what I'd been doing for the last three years, I couldn't really say anything beyond a few unfinished courses, a few failed attempts at University. That's about it. I was a waitress for three months. That was good, being around people. But I never really mixed with the others. And I haven't been well, on and off. At least, that's what they say. Depression, disillusion, something like that, although it's never said a lot to me. Terminology. Just words to describe something we think exists. I've kind of drifted, you know. Never quite believing that I'm twenty-four and breathing still. Sometimes I pinch myself, just to check I'm there. You can never be sure.'

She stops. Catches breath. Slow embarrassment burns on her cheeks, but she doesn't care. This man has seen in to her soul. She needn't explain. He already knows.

He laughs. A vague smile pulls at the edges of his mouth. Helen realises, with a kind of sickening dread, that he doesn't know what to say.

'Gosh' he says, finally finding a word, anything, to fill the thickening silence. He looks up at her, and she senses again the comprehension in his eyes. Perhaps he is too shy to put in to words his feelings, she thinks, relieved to find an outlet from her terror. The terror of misjudgement.

'Well, how about you? Where are you off to at this late hour? Are you studying at the moment? His mouth forms an 'o', while he decides which question to answer first.

'Yeah, I'm studying. English Literature at Kings.'

'Really? I started going there, only I had to leave. My head wasn't sorted enough, you know. But it's a great place! A great University.

I know this is very sudden and everything, but would you like to go for a drink some time? I'd like to see you again, if that's all right?'

His look changes. One by one his features droop. She tries to read his expression but it's difficult. Puzzlement, surprise, indifference? She cannot tell. He looks up at her again, his eyes now sharper. Two black cherries on a luminous cake.

'I'm just on my way to meet my girlfriend. Sorry, but I think it's probably best..... I thought you were lost, you see. Or needed money. I didn't mean to suggest anything. Really, I'm very sorry.'

'You have a girlfriend?'

'Yeah.'

'Oh.'

'Sorry.'

He gets up, picks up his bag. He nearly forgets his glasses, sitting on the seat beside him. 'Can't see a thing without these' he says, a little laugh, a quick five fingered grab, and he's gone.

'That's all right' she says, to no one. Turning to see her reflection in the window. Holes in ice.

At Waterloo she gets off. There's a woman, red hair, black coat. She runs across the platform; excited. A flag of red in a sea of passing faces.

The woman stops two inches in front of a man, same height, perhaps a little smaller. Their arms reach out, enfold one another. They are one, suddenly. Complete. A thick body of completeness.

Helen watched for a while, then they disappeared from view, obscured behind the layers of faces. Stranger in this little world of humanity.

Strange, Helen thinks, as she waves for a cab.
Where does one begin?[1]

Where does one begin? Freshers' Week, September 2007. British universities have (or had in those days, anyway) a reputation for hard drinking. Sussex was no exception. Young people, nearly all strangers to each other, meeting up and living together, is bound to be a stressful situation. From phone calls we had with you, in the following days, it was clear you were struggling. Struggling with the numbers of people you encountered. Struggling to relate to them and struggling to deal with the drinking and drugs culture. We hoped that, once Freshers' Week was over and normal studying began, you would find a routine and life would calm down.

To some extent it did. However, from your perspective, the lectures were large and threatening compared with Birkbeck. Seminars groups were only twelve but you were chronically shy. You had never had the confidence to stand up and speak in a class. When forced to you panicked and fled the room. Your tutor did finally understand this. But worse, most communication with tutors was online. Technology and you had never got on. You needed face to face, one to one – recognition, reassurance as had happened at Birkbeck.

Your contributions in tutorials may have been sparse but some of your writing impressed your tutors. One essay in particular caught the imagination. Amongst the modern novels your tutor group studied was JM Coetzee's *Disgrace*. The novel is set in post-apartheid South Africa. It involves a very flawed central character, David Lurie, a white university lecturer in his fifties. He lectures in Romantic English Literature, Byron, Keats, etc. He

---

1   'The Incomplete', short story by Colette, aged twenty-four.

is an intellectual snob who hasn't fulfilled his ambitions. Twice divorced, he is also contemptuous of women. He gets suspended from the university for sexually exploiting a young female student. He takes refuge on his lesbian daughter's farm up country, and comes into conflict with the local Zulu community there. The story involves what appear to be his unreconstructed racist and sexist views.

When your tutor group was asked to write about Lurie, not surprisingly most wrote about the sexual and/or racial politics in his life, in modern South Africa. You chose a different path. Here's an extract from your essay:

> Where is he, her Byron? Byron is lost, ... And she is lost too, the Teresa he loved, the girl of nineteen...who gave herself up...to the imperious Englishman... [J.M Coetzee, Disgrace, page 182]

You go on to conclude:

> Professor Lurie in Coetzee's 'Disgrace' involved himself with the story of Byron's life and felt able, albeit temporarily, to transport himself to that time and place.

You were alone, amongst your tutor group, in linking Lurie's sexual behaviour to that of Byron, whom he lectured on. The novel is an exploration of South Africa's contemporary social and political conflict but this didn't interest you. Your knowledge of the country's history was pretty sketchy. Anyway none of the racial, social or even sexual politics fired your imagination. I asked you why you concentrated on what seems a minor strand in the novel, rather than the obvious main social issues.

'Were you just trying to be different?'

'Different? No it was the only way, it was obvious Dad. Lurie identified with Byron. That's why he did what he did.'

It proved to be a shrewd line to take as your tutor gave you top marks for the essay. Deservedly, as it is a well-argued piece. However, you were finding the course very unsatisfactory. Most importantly, you made no friends amongst your fellow students. The casual eating habits of students bewildered you. They would meet up and eat pizzas or whatever at random times, like mid-afternoon. For you this was really scary. So, when asked to join them, you would make excuses and go off on a walk alone.

Sharing the campus flat was hard for you too. You each had a shelf in the communal fridge for your food. The others didn't know about your eating disorder. Sometimes you would get back late having drunk but not eaten. The hunger pangs would hit you with a vengeance. You ate food from your flatmates' shelves. You intended to replace it, but good intentions...? Your female flatmate in particular got very angry about it. There was a row. You stopped eating in the kitchen. You ate in your room alone. Your life became enclosed and cut off once again. You were living on a campus with thousands of other young people but you were alone. Once again university was not like your dream. The jigsaw pieces didn't fit.

Amanda and I had moved on with our project. We had renovated much of the semi-ruin we'd bought in France. We had sold our London house and bought a small two-bedroom flat. We talked to you on the phone most days. I had moved on from being purely an actor to also writing TV scripts and plays. So I came over and stayed in our London flat for a week or so each month to have meetings with producers, script editors and my co-writer, and oldest friend, John Flanagan. I would visit you in Brighton. It was all part of trying to have a more adult relationship with you as our grown-up daughter. However, it was clear you weren't happy. Once again it was your isolation that worried us.

You came out to France to have a family Christmas with us. We had a New Year's Eve party. Mainly our age group but of course you'd met many of them on previous visits, and you mingled easily among them. In many ways you got on better with our friends than your own peer group. A number of guests remarked on how much more confident you'd become. And you did meet one young man of your age group who you got on well with. You came out again for the Easter holidays and that also went well...

I've come back to this place
Where countless summers spent,
I'd walk for miles in scorching heat
And sat with aftermath of burning on my cheek.
I've come back to this place
Where countless winters
We'd collect the logs for evening fires,
And in the day traverse the snow gleamed wood till
    tired
I've come back,
And I'm not the same.
But in the sun that bathes my face,
Or the trees who stir their frozen branches
At my tread, I sense that I'm
Returning to simplicity of youthful days.
And holidays
With family and ritual,
And being part of something larger than myself.
I dread to leave, again,
And make this time another distant memory.

But though I wander, happy in my solitude;
Happy in communion with birds and grass and salut-
     ing trees,
I find myself odd moments thinking back to streets
And shops and animated crowds.
Even the roads, swollen with their traffic, hold a special
     awe for me.
But strangely I have found that,
Once I'm settled in one place of living,
The other from which I've fled persuades me back.
I've come back,
Repeated myself, and keep repeating, as nature does
     each time.[2]

That poem while tinged with doubts shows a much more mature attitude to life. It also shows a surprising self-knowledge, in acknowledging that you 'keep repeating'. We continued to worry about your mental state but felt you were making progress. You'd also made a friend on the Sussex campus. Celia (not her real name) was also studying English. She suggested that the pair of you link up with some others she knew, and look for a house or flat to share with them in the second year. (Students have to move out of Halls after their first year and find accommodation off campus.) Celia reasoned that if you went in with quite a few students, you should find a bigger, better property. We were concerned that you'd find sharing, with a lot of strangers, very difficult. We crossed our fingers that it would work out...

---

2   'Going Back' by Colette, 2008.

CHAPTER 14

Number Two, Hove

You also had your concerns. You wrote to your best friend, Caroline Spray, from your days in the Bethlem:

I'm full of concerns about moving in with them, to be honest, although it is exciting and I'm relieved I won't be living on my own again. I was 'dumped' by x2 girls I thought I was to move in with next year. That happened about a month ago. I was gutted. They said it was because they preferred it 'just to be the two of them!' - I don't speak to them anymore. It was 'rejection' in its most poignant, uncompromising form!

So, as you can imagine meeting these people, and being offered a room, came as a real surprise + indeed relief. - But I'm worried that I will never 'fi t- in' the way they all do with one another. I try to act natural, but I always get the sense they feel I'm not so much 'one of them.'

You were right to be worried. The other sharers decided you would not fit in and said there was no longer a place for you. The summer semester was coming to an end. You were homeless. But Celia said she wouldn't take her place in the house if you weren't included. It was apparent that she also had her issues with the guys who were organising the share.

You and Celia seemed to get on. Like you she was a bit of an oddball. She talked a confident case, but again like you, she didn't really have close friends. Maybe two loners together might work? You scoured the estate agents and viewed various properties. Finally it was you who found the mansion flat in upmarket Hove. A 1960s-ish, purpose-built apartment block, on a main road half a mile up from the seafront. Most of the residents were middle aged, some retired. The atmosphere was sedate and stuffy. Not exactly student territory. Flat 2 was on the ground floor. The rooms were spacious. You liked that. No low sloping, claustrophobic ceilings. You and Celia signed the lease with the estate agent. Now you had the keys to your new home and the future. You were proud of your achievement.

But now you had to get all your clobber over from your vacation room on the campus. Celia had gone home to see her parents, before moving in. You couldn't wait. You decided to move on a day that we weren't able to be there to help. We asked our friend Des, who lived in nearby Lewes, if he would drive you over to Hove with your belongings. He readily agreed, in return you agreed to have everything packed and primed to go.

Des arrived on the campus with his son Fergal, a strapping teenager, in tow to help. A wise precaution as it turned out. You of course were not packed or primed but, in fact, in a total mess. An end-of-semester hangover was evident. However, Des and Fergal, with some assistance from you, managed to collect all your various clothes, books, computer, CD player, etc. from the room and pile them into his car. Breathing heavily from the exertion, Des sat behind the wheel and looked across to you sitting contentedly in the front passenger seat.

'Well young Colette,' Des smiled as he gunned the engine, 'and now where are we headed?'

'Sorry?' you respond.

'This new flat of yours, where is it we're taking all this?'

'Oh, I see... It's in Hove Des.'

'Yes, Hove... But what is the actual address Colette?'

'It's number two,' you reply firmly.

A short but significant pause.

'I see, number two, Hove. And that's it?' You nod vigorously.

Des regards you with impassive eyes. 'Are you sure there was not a bit more to the address than just number two, Colette?'

You stare back at him blankly. Impasse. The estate agent has to be traced. The address is eventually extracted. Des finally arrives at the mansion block and delivers you and your belongings to the door of a ground floor flat, with the number two on it.

'You see, I was right Des, it is number two.' A look of triumph flickers in your eyes. Des smiles. It's lucky that he likes you.

We laughed when Des related the tale to us the next day. We all assumed it was just part of your lack of interest in boring practicalities. However, in hindsight, was it not your autism manifesting itself? You never had much sense of direction. You were always getting lost. You had no idea where Hove was, let alone the flat, which you had only visited twice, with Celia guiding you both. The same young woman who wrote the perceptive poem 'Going Back' hadn't even thought about the consequences of having no idea what her new address was. Throughout your life, consequences were something you seemed unable to take on-board. I didn't understand how you could write in such a lucid, adult manner, yet still be so childlike about normal life. Amanda and I learned later, in the light of your diagnosis, that autistic people often lack 'executive function' in the brain. In other words, they don't make certain connections as 'normal' people do. Your confusion over the flat address was, I think, an example of just that.

Most of your tenancy in the new flat, however, was to prove problematic. Hove is some distance from the university, so you had even less social contact. You were becoming disenchanted with Academia. Your more urgent quest was to find a boyfriend, your dream man, who would understand and love you. You'd made no friends apart from Celia and she wasn't interested in seeking out men. Your inability to read people, understand their true feelings about you, was bound to present real problems. Celia was deeply religious. She saw you as someone she could save from sin, not someone to go out on the pull with. You hadn't joined any clubs or societies on campus, so had no reason to go there in the evenings. To overcome your isolation, you tried an online dating site. You had discovered sex with Inis in London. It was the one way you could make relationships. Like many people with mental health issues, you had low self-esteem. Men telling you that you were pretty, buying you drinks and asking you to sleep with them, made you feel good. Most were just using the dating site for casual encounters:

> He wouldn't buy me wine.
> Said it was too strong
> Considering I was already gone.
> So he bought me Stella
> In a bottle, like for a fella,
> And as I tipped it down
> He put his fingers on my throat.
> Touched me so gentle
> And in a way I almost felt myself to sway.

You would never see their chat up lines for what they were – a bit of fun, for one night only. You believed their passionate protestations of admiration. You would always end up disappointed.

> But you left me cold and dry.
> Asked for my number, but you didn't reply.
> So I sit, now, in my flat
> And pour endless glasses of wine that I hate,
> And entertain thoughts of meeting you
> Randomly
> In an unasked for way
> As I go about being successful and great.[1]

After one dumping too many, you reverted to self-harm. Celia disapproved of your behaviour; both the online men and the self-harm. She was determined to control your behaviour. Her reaction was extreme. She would lock you in your bedroom, to prevent you from going out on dates. Of course this led to rows between you. Beneath your shy exterior there was a fierce and very angry little person. The atmosphere in the flat became toxic.

You came and stayed with us in London for a family Christmas. Chloe and Teddy had had their first child, Ollie, at the beginning of the year. So it was a Christmas celebrating our enlarged family, for the first time. It went well, as I recall. On 29th December Amanda drove you back to Brighton with your presents. You wanted 'to get back to your own space' you said. She left you at your flat around 4.30 pm. Celia was still away. Then what happened was to become a template for future behaviour. Having wanted to be on your own, very quickly a cloud descended. Your mood darkened. You went out for a drink and

---

1   From an untitled poem by Colette, 2009.

to buy provisions. You came home and put food in a pan onto a gas hob. Having drunk too much wine, you lay down on your bed and fell asleep. The contents of the pan overheated and started a fire. The kitchen filled with smoke. You were out for the count. Fortunately a neighbour, in the block of flats opposite, saw the flames. By the time the Fire Brigade arrived your flat was filled with smoke. An ambulance took you into A&E. You were asked whether it had been a suicide attempt. Obviously, with your mental health record, that had to be a possibility. You were kept in overnight.

The hospital phoned Amanda. You'd left your mobile in your flat, so you gave them your mum's mobile number. It was the only one you always remembered. We were horrified to hear about the fire. But for that neighbour you could have died. Only hours earlier you'd seemed to be fine. We accepted your word that it was a complete accident; but Amanda had only left you a couple of hours earlier. Why had your mood plummeted like that?

Several years later, when you were diagnosed as being on the spectrum, the psychologist said, 'Colette, tell your mum and dad how you feel when they leave you.'

'Well, they're there. And then they're gone. As if they've gone behind a curtain. It's like a black cloud. I'm alone…and there's nothing.'

We looked to you, realising that we'd had no idea you'd seen our partings in that light. Hearing this, we did understand better, but sadly that meeting wasn't until you were thirty-three years old.

Back in 2009, after the fire, other residents at Grove Court wanted you students to be evicted. However, the police and Fire Brigade accepted that it had been an accident. Meanwhile Celia got back and understandably was very upset. She took your mobile phone and erased all your numbers. She called us, in quite a state. She asked us to have you sectioned, saying it would be for your own good. I explained to her that wasn't how sectioning worked. The doctors at the hospital had already assessed you and sent you home. The decision was theirs and had been taken. I suggested that Celia should give you back your phone at once. This was a tipping point in the relationship between you.

Your second year was looking more and more fraught. We encouraged you to consult the university counselling service. You followed our advice, which was unusual. You were suspicious of all medics by this time, so you must have been desperate for support. You got to all your weekly appointments with your new counsellor. When the agreed ten-week programme finished, she wrote to you. She said that she thought you had serious psychological problems that were too complicated for her, or the counselling service, to treat. In her opinion, you should take time out of university and move into a supportive psychological community. She suggested a couple of places. They were hundreds of miles away. That was the limit of the help offered. You were signed off.

While the counsellor's assessment was honest, there was no follow-up. Realistically you weren't going to take a year out of university and go into a therapeutic commune. We tried to discuss it.

'Therapeutic community!? Back into an institution! After all those years in hospital. Never, no way!'

But you did agree to consult your GP on the campus. Amanda went with you. He was shown the counsellor's letter. He was cold and brusque. When told of your self-harming he was unsympathetic. He refused to refer you on to a psychiatrist and merely suggested that you should pull yourself together. So...nobody to consult, and nowhere to go.

You've put me in a place where I cannot access help,
Because I loathe the way you talk at me.
Textbook - style.
As if you know my every thought and feeling,
Telling me I know nothing of the origins of my illness.
How stupid you are
For not knowing the stupidity of your curt remarks.
How far off the mark you were,
When you sat there,
Smug with self- conceited pride;
So sure you knew the inner workings of my mind.
What fools!!!![2]

We understand that university mental health provision has improved in the last ten years. Organisations like Brain in Hand support many undergraduates. However, even as I write in 2020, we still regularly read about students becoming suicidal. Avoidable deaths appear to be commonplace. We have encountered many such cases through our contacts with the charity Inquest, which does amazing and vital work on behalf of bereaved families. The truth is there is nothing like sufficient support for mental health in universities, or anywhere else in this country. Over the last ten years, successive health secretaries have promised to put mental health on an equal footing with physical health. In reality, all their anodyne words turn out to be false and all their promised funding evaporates. Mental health facilities and buildings are frequently run-down and unfit for purpose. There is a chronic shortage of mental health doctors, thus waiting times for ASD diagnosis are getting longer and longer. Now it is often between one and two years. Staff within

2   From 'Fear' by Colette.

the clinics are not adequately trained or qualified and always under stress. Thus the needs of mental health patients are not met and the situation is only getting worse.

In your case, you had had a narrow escape, with the fire. The flat share was proving to be a disaster. You were only half-way through the second year of your degree. We couldn't see how you were going to complete it. Then help came from an unexpected source...

CHAPTER 15

Online Fishing

Given your disinterest in computers, I was surprised how you took to online dating. But of course for someone as shy as you were, it cut out a lot of awkward early manoeuvring. Your website promised plenty of choice of potential partners. However, as you told it, the quality of partner didn't always match up. Men claiming to be cool, and interesting, turned out to be only interested in one thing. Men, who posted photos resembling Johnny Depp, turned out to look more like Homer Simpson through a fisheye lens. However, as with a stopped clock, eventually the website got it right. Jamie (not his real name) came all the way down from the Midlands to meet you. The date must have been a success. He came down again and again.

While slightly younger than you, Jamie was already a graduate. He had a degree from a good university. He'd returned to the Derby area where he grew up and was finding it hard to get employment of any sort there. When he visited you, he fell in love with Brighton very quickly. It was young, fun and lively. He was, I think, equally taken with you. He came across as bright and a good guy. He was the first boyfriend of yours that we actually met. You both seemed happy and easy with each other. Living over two-hundred miles apart was a problem but then again maybe the distance would give you space to get to know each other.

Celia was not happy about it. Jamie would spend long weekends in the flat with you. You watched DVDs of *Peep Show*, drinking beer and eating takeaways while hooting with laughter. Celia not only disapproved of you taking over the TV and living room but also that you would go to bed together at any hour of the day. When Jamie made his trips down to stay, the pair of you were inseparable. I think you were genuinely in love. But his presence in the flat drove a further wedge between you and Celia. It was coming to the end of your second year at Sussex. Jamie, having already completed a degree course, encouraged you to engage more with your tutors. You did enough work to pass your end-of-year exams, meaning you could move on to your final year.

The lease on the flat was soon to run out. There was no question of extending it. There was also no question of you and Celia sharing again. Jamie suggested that he move down from Derby and that you live together. It would be easier for him to find work in Sussex than it was back up in Derbyshire. You could find a one-bedroom flat. With both of you paying rent, you should be able to manage it. It was a big step for Jamie. You were the only person he knew in Brighton; all his family and friends were hundreds of miles away. However, it was clear that this was what you both wanted. When we discussed it with you, you were quite confident about the plans. You told us you loved him. You had by now known each other for nearly six months. It did seem a genuinely positive move for you. It could bring stability to your life and Jamie would have a much better chance of finding employment. So we offered to help with deposits, etc. and that summer you, Jamie, Amanda and I searched for a flat to rent.

Self-portrait in black and red hat

Albert Bridge

Green/yellow/blue self-portrait

Andy and Col, aged four, on holiday in Greece

Col and older sister Chloe, aged ten and fifteen

Col just out of adolescent unit, aged thirteen

Col in leather jacket, aged fifteen

Col under lime tree in France, aged twenty-six

Col, aged twenty-eight, and nephew Ollie, aged three, at Christmas time

Colette's nightmares

We found one in a quiet street close to Brighton's London Road Station. Much more of a student area than Hove. The flat consisted of a small bedroom, equally small living room, kitchenette and bathroom. It was at the top of the Victorian house. It was in reasonable condition. Youngish tenants occupied the two flats below. Trains from London Road Station went direct to the university. You were happy. Jamie was happy. The flat was taken, the lease in your name alone. Jamie went back home. A date was fixed for when he would arrive with his stuff. You were to meet him. But when the day came, you went missing.

Jamie arrived in Brighton and you weren't at the station as had been arranged. Your mobile seemed to be switched off. He phoned us. We were in London and couldn't raise you either. Eventually, you called us back. We had a garbled conversation. You said you were with friends. You wouldn't say who they were or where you were. The background noise sounded like a pub. Jamie had no keys to the flat yet. He was left stranded and bewildered at Brighton Station. Initially we were equally baffled. You'd said you loved him. Why would you stand him up like this?

In retrospect, we realise that you must have been in a blind panic. For the first time since you and Jamie had decided to live together, it dawned on you what a massive adjustment this would be to your life. You'd never been able to share a flat successfully with anyone. Now you were to share a new home with some guy who'd be there all the time; someone who would also be sharing your bathroom, your kitchen and your bed. You were facing the biggest upheaval in your adult existence. We didn't get it then but we realise now that your autistic mind went into near meltdown at the prospect. To repeat, autistic people find change of any sort very hard. You wanted to be with Jamie but I think the reality hadn't hit you, until this moment. As you wrote:

Treading on thin ice again
So scared I can hardly breathe
Trying to make up for lost time
With hand outstretched and eyes wide shut
I'd better mind my step,
or the world will come thundering around my ears.
I'd better mind my step,
or I'll be sorry when the 'chips are down'.[1]

It was another six hours before you called him and met up. It is a credit to Jamie that he didn't harbour any hard feelings. Then as the autumn semester started your lives settled into an easier routine. Jamie got a short-term job that paid just about enough. You found the journey in from London Road to the campus much easier than from Hove. Your attendance improved. Jamie helped you with your essay plans. You cooked together. You watched *Peep Show* together. You appeared to have worked out a way of life together. Things were looking a lot more hopeful.

Christmas 2009. We asked you and Jamie down to France for the holiday. Chloe, Teddy and their now two children, Ollie and Sam, were also coming. Chloe's children were young to bring on a plane but she was determined. She felt that this Christmas was important to her and the whole family. She booked a flight to Toulouse. You were too late to get seats on the same flight but managed to book a later one, the same day. It all seemed to be falling into place. Chloe would be there with her partner and her two little boys. You, with your boyfriend Jamie, would be there as an equal adult. It was going to be the first time we'd all been together for a family Christmas for a very long time. We were holding our breath – would it all work out?

---

1   An untitled piece by Colette.

You were all flying out on 22nd December. The night of the 21st, blizzards hit London. The runways at Gatwick and Heathrow were blocked with snow. There was massive disruption. Chloe and her family got to the airport. Her flight was cancelled. Not a hope in hell of another one this side of Christmas. She tried Eurostar. The Tunnel was also blocked. There seemed to be nothing she could do. She was devastated. She had a nasty cold and was very tired. She was desperate to get away. So she and Teddy decided to hire a car at any cost and drive down, crossing the channel by ferry. Teddy doesn't drive, so Chloe would have all that in front of her. We tried to dissuade her but she said that this holiday was far too important.

Frantic arrangements were being put into place in France and London. A ferry was booked for that evening. We reserved a hotel room in Boulogne for the family to stay in that night. I booked a morning train to Châteauroux, halfway to Boulogne. I would meet them there and take over the driving. It is over six-hundred miles from Boulogne to us. Chloe's cold was developing into what seemed like flu.

Meanwhile what of you and Jamie? It seemed you'd been sprinkled with lucky Christmas stardust. Blissfully unaware of all the panic, you made your way that afternoon to Gatwick. The snow had been cleared. You called to say, quite angrily, that your flight had been delayed for an hour! I drove into collect you and Jamie and take you back to our house. You were rather pleased with yourself getting there before your sister. The next morning I took the train north and collected your exhausted sister and her family. Chloe took Christmas Eve to recover, and then we had what Amanda and I recall as our best Christmas Day ever. Our two daughters were together and happy. Teddy is a brilliant cook and created a fantastic meal. He and Jamie got on fine. Extravagant presents were exchanged. Local wine was drunk. Bad jokes and old stories told. Over the ten days, we had long walks through the snow blanketed forests, evenings watching films on our home cinema, the wood burner blazing. Long discussions and much nonsense talked. Always present the laughter, shrieks and cries of two very young, over excited grandchildren. Joy was in the air, a feeling that everything was going to be all right. It was to be the best of times...sadly never to be repeated.

The relative calm of your life with Jamie, over the last six months, was about to be tested. Dark clouds were gathering, rumbling thunder could be heard. As with any storm, it was to be a combination of different elements that would cause the unravelling of your relationship. After the Christmas break in France, Jamie returned to Brighton and unemployment. Despite searching and temping for six months, he found himself jobless. He had no money. He didn't know anyone in the town. Your relationship was built on mutual sexual attraction and a shared sense of humour. Unfortunately now the laughter had died for both of you. As for you, your finals were approaching, you were well behind with your dissertation and, as with your GCSEs and A-Levels, you were beginning to panic. You told Jamie you couldn't work in the claustrophobic atmosphere of the flat. Despite of all your own problems, you seemed unable to empathise with his. You said you would have to work in the library instead. But, with so little supervision from the English department, you lost your way. Once again you had no one to turn to. This time your boyfriend couldn't help. So what did you do? You went off and had a one-night stand with a student who lived nearby.

You phoned your mum and told her about it. You said you must tell Jamie what you'd done.

'Col, you did this on the spur of the moment. You're not going to do it again, it was just an angry reaction?'

'Suppose so, yeah.'

'Then don't tell Jamie. He'd be incredibly hurt. Say nothing – he's having a tough enough time already, he doesn't need it,' Amanda reasoned.

'No Ma, I have to be honest, I have to tell him,' you responded.

I don't think that being honest was the real reason why you told Jamie. You'd always had to take matters to the wire. It was as if you needed to know the limits of people's tolerance. Testing just how much they really cared for you? And once they snapped and rejected you, it would only prove that you really were worthless. That you were right to hold yourself in such low self-esteem. If they didn't snap, you felt impelled to push the crisis further until they did. A pattern that would continue through your life:

> And then I guess I pushed the privileges too far.
> The nights I didn't turn up and you
> Left smoking weed in need to sleep
> Away thoughts of what I was doing instead.
> And you told me it was over
> When I was drunk and acting o'hara-esk.
> I never believed you.
> It took two weeks of your hate to make me realise
> I had killed your love.
> And it made me think how strange it is
> That our perceptions can change so much
> Given time
> And that I had been beautiful to you
> But the same eyes and mouth
> no longer spoke the volumes they did
> Because I was me
> And you did not like me.[2]

---

2   From 'On You Saying No' by Colette, 2009.

It was the end for Jamie, he was shattered. You begged him for forgiveness but it was too late.

He left and went back to Derbyshire. You called him and pestered him on the phone. You went up by train to try and persuade him back. He treated you with cold contempt and anger.

You were alone once more, facing an unfinished dissertation and your finals. Under the circumstances, you did surprisingly well in your exams. You would have achieved a 2:1. But you never managed to finish your dissertation, so your degree was unfinished. In itself, that was unimportant. What mattered was that you were cut loose and rudderless again. Leaving university was to be an ominous turning point in your life. Now you had no structure, no boyfriend, no psychological support and no purpose. It was what you had always feared, 'the nothing'. You were alone...and you couldn't be alone. But you also couldn't 'be' with anyone. You were facing the void...

Part III

CHAPTER 16

The Void Beckons

It was 2009. Seismic shifts were taking place. We, like most others, hadn't taken in their full implications. The world had been evolving while we sleepwalked through our everyday lives. It was becoming a much darker, hostile place. The old post-war certitudes, the NHS, the welfare state had long been crumbling, just as buildings that receive no maintenance crumble. But now, post the Lehman Brothers crash in 2008, the landlords of the state set about a systemic demolition process. Piece by piece the components of the welfare state were put out to tender or neglected and left to wither away. Previously state-funded places of refuge, where those in need had taken shelter and received care, disappeared. Social care evaporated before our eyes. We were told that this was a crisis. Sacrifices had to made. But somehow it was never the casino bankers, who'd caused the disaster, that were to make the sacrifices. Nor was it the government. It was the rest of us, who were just trying to get on with our lives. Government politicians told us all would be well if we accepted the cuts. A short spell of pain and then we would reach the sunlit uplands. We knew they were lying but what could be done? *The Guardian* journalist Polly Toynbee wrote at the time words to the effect of: With this new government, don't be old, don't be poor, don't be unemployed, don't be ill. You had no interest in politics but some of your writing was remarkably apposite:

> I wander on this brick paved pain,
> A shattered landscape out of frame.
> Wherever treading needles rise
> To scratch and prick and cause my cries.
> When once a curious adventurer I
> Embarked this journey, now defy
> With all my needs clung at my side
> I started down this slippery slide.[1]

The world you stepped out into after university was brutal and it was fast getting more brutal. You got a 'job' in telephone sales. You weren't paid a salary, nor did you have any employment rights. You only received money when you talked some mug into buying whatever useless product the company was flogging. Initially you made a couple of sales. You were cock-a-hoop, you told us that you were so happy that you danced a little jig. Then the next three days nothing. You decided to alter their banal sales script; you were sure you could do better. Day four your supervisor spots the new salesgirl spouting some strange script into the phone:

'What are you at young lady, that's not our sales pitch?'

'No I know it's not. I'm making it more interesting you see... well it is really boring isn't it.'

The next morning you arrived to find your services were no longer required. You were indignant. You got an interview for a job as a waitress. But you became so anxious that morning, you couldn't even leave your flat, let alone get to the café. We

---

1   From 'The Road' by Colette.

knew that, with your fragile mental health, a full-time job would
be a near impossibility. You had no practical qualifications. We
helped you look for a course at Brighton Metropolitan College
which might lead to something. You said you fancied taking
a BTEC in Beauty Therapy. You insisted it was something that
interested you.

Meantime you signed on for Jobseeker's Allowance. As I
recall, it was a bit under £60 per week. We took you to register
with a GP in Brighton. The practice seemed very helpful and
friendly. Your medical notes from the university doctors were
passed on. But they turned out to be only your recent medical
history; no details of the eating disorder years. We visited your
GP with you a number of times. We explained your mental health
history. He sighed and told us, with genuine regret in his voice,
that there was a massive waiting list. You wouldn't get to see a
psychiatrist for at least a year. And as for Cognitive Behavioural
Therapy (CBT), which medics felt would help you, that was a
two-year wait. Your poem continues:

> I did not know what I know now,
> Would not know what, with whom or how.
> My thoughts were bent on future aims
> With little knowledge of their pains.
> The road ahead looks punishing hard,
> Its benefits seem strangely marred.
> Is this the road that's meant for me?
> The only way to set me free?[2]

You wrote 'Road' some years earlier, at a similar moment of
change in your life. In previous crises someone or something

---

2   From Col's poem 'Road'.

had always turned up to alleviate the problem. But this time, in August 2010, you met Dave (not his real name)...

You had arranged to spend an evening with a couple of girls from the telephone sales team. They didn't show up. You headed for a late-night takeaway pizza on your own. Dave was waiting in the pizza delivery shop when you made your order, you told us. I met him some weeks later with you. He was around fifty years old, with a grey thinning, scraped back ponytail. Below average height with a boozer's crashed in face, narrow eyes, but a mischievous smile. He engaged you with some chat about 'two for the price of one pizzas'. You took two pizzas and Dave home with you. You were lonely having been stood up by your supposed friends. It was only a few days before Dave was moving his stuff into your flat.

Unable to make everyday friendships, you turned to your only method of making relationships. Sex. Relationships for you had to be almost instantaneous. The idea of building a deeper understanding of each other, before plunging in, didn't occur to you. Up until now most of your boyfriends had been of your own age group and most were students. With Dave you were entering a different culture. He was old enough to be your father. He in fact had a daughter not much younger than you. He was twice divorced. He had a criminal record. He lived off benefits, cash-paid removal work and petty theft. He had been staying in downmarket hostels until he met you at the takeaway. We only found all this out gradually from you, when it was far too late.

Meanwhile, as the new academic year began, you enrolled for your part-time Beauty Therapy course. The night before your second day, you had your first major row with Dave. You had both been drinking heavily. I don't think you knew exactly what started it. He hated you using long words, words he didn't understand.

'Think you're so clever, can't even find the dole office without me taking you.'

But you knew how to hit back and go for his jugular:

'I'm stupid?! What about that dumb daughter of yours, too thick to write her own name!'

You knew Dave's daughter was his Achilles heel. He hit you hard across the face. You passed out on the bed. Your left eye was throbbing. You woke to see it had turned dark purple and closed up. You dashed out for a taxi to the Eye Hospital, terrified you'd lost your sight in that eye. Dave rushed after you on foot, scared you'd report him to the police.

In the morning you were discharged. No damage had been done to the retina but you had a whopping great black eye and bruised face. All your GP could offer was that you attend self-help groups for abused women and alcohol dependency. The college said that you couldn't continue the beauty course in that state. Your hands were shaking, your face was swollen; you were all over the place. We reasoned with you. A man who hits you is dangerous, you have to insist that Dave leaves your flat. If he doesn't go, you must report him to the police. You said you would but you didn't. You were both drinking a lot of vodka, sometimes from early in the day. We would call you sometimes in the late morning and you would still be in bed saying you were feeling ill. The rows between you became more and more frequent. The neighbours downstairs complained to the landlord. They wanted you to be evicted.

You started asking us for money. It turned out he didn't just take you to sign on, he took your benefit as well. Or talked you into giving him it. Same thing. But it transpired that Dave had a longer-term plan than just nicking your Jobseeker's Allowance. You told us that he was trying to get you pregnant. Said he wanted to have a baby with you. He told you that if you did, you'd be able to get a council flat. You were really excited by the plan. You said it was your dream to have a child.

'Chloe has two children, why shouldn't I have one?' you proclaimed into your mobile.

We tried to explain why it was such a bad idea. 'He already has several children. Never looked after any of them. It'd be irresponsible Col.'

'You're hypocrites! Just don't like him coz he's not educated, like you!'

'No Col, it's his drinking and violence. And you'd have nowhere to bring up a child. He's talking nonsense, no way you'd get a council flat. Waiting list in Brighton is years.'

'A baby is my heart's desire and you two just wanna stop me. Well you can't.'[3]

It was nearly Christmas. Chloe asked you up to London to stay with her and her family. Dave wouldn't let you go. He said, 'I can't be alone babe, it's Christmas.' Chloe was very supportive of you. She told you that her door was always open and you could come at any time – but not if you brought a violent boyfriend with you. She had two little boys and that just wasn't on.

Dave's scheme to make you pregnant concerned us deeply. You had always refused to use the contraceptive pill because it would make you fat. You had relied on your boyfriends using condoms. Pregnancy had always been a risk. Now that risk had become a stark reality. Early in January I was in London. I decided I must go to Brighton and talk to you both. The plan to have a child must be seriously discussed. The drinking and the rowing had to stop or you'd be on the streets. Dave must move out and get his own place. I phoned you and arranged to meet at your flat. I arrived at around 9 am, the agreed time. I rang the

---

3 Heart's desire was typical of the sort of Victorian style she often used.

bell. No answer. I got your nearest neighbour (who liked you) to let me into the building. I knocked on your flat door. No answer again. I rang your mobile. No answer once more. But I could hear its ringtone coming from within the flat. I was now worried. Furious at my coming to interfere had Dave lashed out and really hurt you? I called the police. They smashed open the door. The flat was empty. Your phone was on the floor by your bed. I was very puzzled. You knew I was coming. We'd talked only last night on the phone. Where on earth were you? I thanked the police for their help. They left. I pondered the broken door lock and my missing daughter.

You eventually turned up an hour later. You had woken up and remembered it was signing-on day at the job centre. You'd dashed out forgetting your phone. You said you'd kicked Dave out the night before. Then you noticed your smashed open door for the first time. Your eyes widened in disbelief.

'What the fuck Dad!? What've you done? What'll the landlord say!?'

You had a way of shifting the blame from yourself onto who-ever else was around. In this case, me. However, I explained to you how worried I'd been. The police were already aware of your address because of neighbours' complaints about the domestic rows; they hadn't needed much encouragement to come round. Dave was very much 'known to them' as well. So now, I insist-ed that you and I go to the police station and have the address officially marked. Then you could report him any time he tried to get into your flat again. Once that was done, we would get your door mended and put a new lock on it. You were reluctant but agreed. The cops took a statement from you and told you to contact them immediately if Dave tried to get in. An injunction was taken out stopping Dave from approaching you in the street or going to your flat.

I reassured you that I would stay to ensure that Dave was kept out. Amanda came over and we stayed with our very close friends, Caroline and Edmond O'Reilly, who lived in the city. Theirs was an oasis for us.

I left you the night after you had kicked Dave out, very late. He was apparently watching the flat. As soon as I'd gone he rang your mobile and talked his way back in. When I found out the next morning I called the police. Dave was arrested and then let go. The pattern repeated itself a couple of times over the weekend. I couldn't believe that you kept letting him back in. I shouldn't have been surprised; you were only behaving as many abused women do.

On Monday you told the police that Dave had recently attempted to rape you. We were taken that afternoon to Crawley Hospital. Sussex Police had a forensic facility there for cases like this. Nurses and medics physically examined you, photographing the bruising on your upper thighs, etc. The bruising turned out to be some days old but extensive. The process took hours. It was extremely disturbing and upsetting for you. Why hadn't you told me about this? I only found your short story some years later:

The tears come back but I'm making no noise. Hot relief-full tears. They feel good. Feel like I'm shedding the weight of my actions, of my misdeeds, of my life. I am not me, not this. It never happened. I will get up soon and I will see it was a bad dream and I'm back in my flat and the sun is out and I am looking forward to normal things, like friends I have never had and a job I have never held. Yes, my life, as it should have been, as it isn't, as it never was. My life.[4]

---

4   Excerpt from a short story 'What Happened to Your Face?' by Colette.

I dropped you off at your flat very late that night. On Tuesday morning we went back to the police and you made a lengthy statement to stop Dave approaching you again. That evening, Dave was arrested at the hostel he was now staying in.

On the Wednesday the police suggested that it would be best to charge Dave with assault, not rape. Rape is very difficult to prove in court. The next day Dave was charged on five counts of assault. He was released on bail, on condition that he did not approach you again. I dumped his stuff at his hostel.

Conditions are one thing but enforcing them is quite another. Brighton is a very busy city. The police couldn't keep tabs on Dave. The next four weeks were to be a game of cat and mouse.

Your landlord wanted you out. We were helping you look for an alternative flat, without success. We spent the days going round estate agents, having doctor's appointments and going to voluntary support groups for abused women and alcohol dependency. Nearly every time we dropped you off, Dave would come round within minutes. You often let him in. I realised he must be watching the place. Much of Brighton is built on hillsides. Your street was typical. I scouted all the nearby streets and found a mattress and bedding hidden by a wall. The wall overlooked your street and your front door. I destroyed the mattress.

Amanda took you to the doctor again. You were in great distress. The GP could only offer Valium to calm you down but no further psychological support. There was nothing available. In the six months you had spent with Dave, your drinking had become a serious problem. We now know this was a form of self-medication common amongst people on the autistic spectrum. I include here a quote by Matthew Tinsley from *Asperger Syndrome and Alcohol*:

The chief aspect of my autism which resulted in extremely

heavy use of alcohol to cope was a near constant sense of anxiety. I also was socially awkward and discovered alcohol turned me into a much more relaxed person. Of course, I was unaware of my autism at the time and it's only in retrospect that I can understand why it worked so well.[5]

Of course, you also had no idea you were on the spectrum, nor had we. We thought that after continual heavy drinking with Dave, you'd become physically addicted. There was some truth in that but it was also far from the whole story, as we were to find out.

The local voluntary self-help groups, while well meaning, were of little use. You tried them all from AA (Alcoholics Anonymous) to SLAA (Sex and Love Addiction Anonymous) and many in between. We'd take you to cold church halls and meeting houses. None of them worked for you. Why not?

'You see I gear myself up, I manage to speak. People come up and say well done! ... But I know I can't do it again – I was sort of pretending. So I can't go back.'

I have an old friend who was a counsellor at a specialist addiction clinic in London. You knew him quite well. I called Mike and he talked to you. He asked you if you wanted to stop drinking. You told him you did. He said you needed a change of environment, a kick-start to break your patterns of behaviour. You needed to go into a rehab clinic, dry out and work with the clinic to see a way forward. He knew an excellent place. He had a word with his boss. She concurred with his assessment and called Clouds House. It was near the end of the financial year. They sometimes had spaces for people who needed support, but

5   Tinsley, M. and Hendrickx, S. (2008) *Asperger Syndrome and Alcohol*. London: Jessica Kingsley Publishers.

did not have enough money for the very high fees. Mike and his boss recommended that you should have one of those places. Clouds House agreed but now would you agree to go? One day you said you would, the next day you said you wouldn't. We couldn't believe it, help had been found but it seemed you wouldn't accept it. Then, the following evening, Amanda's mobile rang:

'All right, all right – I'll go.'

'What's made you change your mind love?'

'Well I'm looking at my Subway salad. I'm cold. It's dark. I'm alone – can't be much worse than this can it?'

But, in a pattern we now recognised, saying you would do something and actually doing it were very different things for you. A week later, when the day for admission arrived, we drove round to your flat. You weren't dressed. You hadn't packed. We looked to you questioningly. You weren't having it.

'I'm not going. I won't be locked away again Dad.'

'They don't lock people up. You'll be in a big house with other people like you, everyone there has problems with alcohol.'

'You'll all be grown-ups, you all want to get better. You all help each other, Col,' Amanda reassured.

'Don't both of you start on me! I won't listen, I won't! Anyway I can't leave my room like this. The wardrobe's in the wrong place!'

We looked at the wardrobe. It seemed to be fine where it was. Your OCD was kicking in big time to prevent you doing what you knew you should.

The voices – I am not ordered by some croaky Demon to behave the way I do. An idea flickers across the canvas of my brain. Sometimes the idea gets stuck. It becomes lodged, permanently in a cranny of the mind, as a tiny twig might in a stream. Once it is there it will not budge. I become a twisted knot of pent up energy.[6]

At the time, we didn't understand this. We'd got this far. You had a place at one of the most respected rehab clinics in the country and now you wouldn't take the final step. Amanda signalled to me that she would wait in the car. Sometimes it was better when you only had one of us to deal with. I asked you calmly where the wardrobe should be. You indicated a spot a few inches from where it was. I manoeuvred it over. Then a chair had to be moved. Then a table lamp. Then we sat in silence for some time. Eventually, you started to shove some clothes into a bag.

Half an hour later we emerged out the front door and joined Amanda in the car. You sat in the back, as usual. I started the car and we set off to Clouds House in Wiltshire. You closed your eyes and slept all the way there.

---

6   From Col's autobiography.

CHAPTER 17

All Change

Government austerity, arbitrarily imposed to deal with the banking crisis, led to your health and care services being slashed. And it also had other, unforeseen consequences for our family. Once you left university we realised there was no way you could get by in the outside world, without considerable support. We didn't know why you suffered from such crippling anxiety but it was clear you couldn't hold down a job or build meaningful relationships. We knew that your problems were genuine, but we were lost as to what the root of those problems were.

We abandoned our plans to spend our later years in France. You couldn't live in rural France. You didn't speak French and you didn't drive. Anyway you'd told us in no uncertain terms that you couldn't live with us full time anywhere. So we proposed to sell our now renovated French house and our small London flat. Then we could buy a place with enough room for you to stay as, and when, you felt like it. You said you wanted to continue living in Brighton. You knew the city well now and felt it was your home. We would find somewhere within easy reach so that we could provide support and a refuge when necessary.

'The best laid schemes of mice and men...' Since the crash, the property market in rural France had fallen through the floor.

Where three years earlier people from all over Europe had been escaping the cities for a dream life in calm idyllic countryside, now few buyers were to be found. We put our much-loved home on the market in the spring. By autumn we hadn't had a single enquiry. We were stuck. Another side effect of the financial crash was that most of my script writing commissions dried up. The TV studios, where I'd been doing the majority of my work, closed down. This only added to the pressure on us to cut our expenses and move back full time to the UK. Retirement was off the agenda in France or anywhere else.

Meanwhile, earlier in the year, you'd gone in for four weeks' rehab at Clouds House. I visited you, as did Chloe on a separate occasion. Initially, you had mild withdrawal symptoms coming off the alcohol but that had calmed down in a couple of days. You explained how you all mucked in together, with the cleaning, serving up food and doing chores around the property. You told us all about the twelve-step regime. You said you couldn't deal with the AA concept of the 'Higher Power' but otherwise you were full of enthusiasm for the clinic's philosophy. You took part in the group therapy sessions where people shared their problems and discussed their personal struggles. You got on well with the other 'clients'.

'It's amazing Dad, some of the people here have really good jobs. There's a woman lawyer, a PHD student, an ex soldier... I mean it makes me feel less stupid, gives me hope for the future...'

You chatted on to me over a cup of tea in the canteen. Other residents came up to us and said hello. You were clearly liked. You were looking and feeling physically better than you had for months. But as you told me all this, there was a familiar doubt hanging in the air. You were saying all the things that you knew I'd want to hear. Was this for real? How would you manage when you got back and all the support was gone?

The answer was predictable. Once back in your home environment, in Brighton, you reverted to your old routines. Of course you did, the twelve-step programme, on its own, was not going to work for someone with autism. It couldn't in your case because alcohol addiction was not the root problem. As Mark Brosnan and Sally Adams, from the University of Bath, say in their paper:

> A large population-based cohort study identified that a diagnosis of autism without an intellectual disability is associated with a much higher increased risk of alcohol misuse...

> Most service providers report having received no specific knowledge or skills sessions on autism during their training, and perceive that treatment outcomes for autistic clients are relatively unfavourable compared with other client groups.[1]

But this was 2011 and nobody at Clouds House was aware that you were on the autistic spectrum. As it was, you returned from the clinic. You picked up with Dave again with disastrous results. The drink-fuelled rows and violence resumed. Your downstairs neighbours, after a month of peace when you were away in rehab, were once again being regularly disturbed. They had a young child and they'd had enough. So had the landlord. You were given a month's notice to quit. We put it to the landlord that, given your state of mental health, you needed more time to find another home. We went to your GP with you and explained the crisis. Under the stress of eviction you were self-harming again

---

1   Adams, S. and Brosnan, M. (2019) 'Adapting alcohol support services for autistic people.' National Autistic Society. Accessed on 04/05/2020 at https://network.autism.org.uk/good-practice/evidence-base/adapting-alcohol-support-services-autistic-people.

and frequently ending up in A&E. Your GP was a good doctor. He knew you well enough by now to understand that you had serious mental health problems. But all he was able to do was write you a letter for the landlord and offer more voluntary groups to support you. Apart from filling up your day, the groups were of little help.

At much the same time you were called in by Atos, the private firm working for the Department for Work and Pensions, who review whether unemployed people should continue to qualify for benefit. You missed the first appointment because you got lost and couldn't find the office. The second one was on a Sunday. They were so keen to get people off benefit that they paid staff to work over weekends in specially hired offices. You filled in a twenty-five-page form yourself, without advice. The forms are full of traps and hardly acknowledge psychological problems. So that basically if you can walk, you can work. The 'expert' conducting your review had no experience or qualifications in mental health. Your interview consisted of being asked if you'd been able to get to this appointment without help and whether you could stand on one leg. As you could do both things, you were declared fit to work. You apparently had: 'Zero physical problems. Zero mental health problems.' Unbelievable with your medical record! They told you if you wanted to challenge this decision, you would have to go before a Tribunal.

You got back to the flat and had a massive row with Dave. He was angry that you were to be cut off benefit. He hit you. The police were called and Dave was arrested. After further confrontations with Dave, you gave a three-hour statement to the police. For some weeks the cat-and-mouse chase with him continued. The police would arrest him then let him go. You would let him back in and the violence would start all over again. On one occasion he gagged you and burned your arm with a cigarette butt. You were in and out of A&E for injuries inflicted by Dave and self-harm. Despite seeming almost addicted to checking in there, you had something of a jaundiced view of A&E. At least you did as expressed in this opening excerpt of your short story:

'What Happened to Your Face?'

The question hovers in the air like a bat with no wings, leering at me with its impossible flight. My fingers are snakes turned purple from cold and wringing. I look at her but she makes no sense. Her eyes mutate and become goldfish. Her lips move but not to the shape of her words.
'My face got damaged.'
I didn't think to say that, it travels from me like a scheduled train.
'Are we going to play games today?'
She smiles like a cobra. I wince and look down at the purple wringing snakes in my hollowed lap.
'What I need to understand is, do you actually want to die?'
'I didn't mean to.' I answer quickly and avoid her gaze because I'm not liking her much. Why no kindness? Why?
'I don't know, I just find it hard to live.'
A pathetic whimper, it almost makes me angry. Get up and scream; Don't ask me questions I cannot answer bitch! Truth peers at me from a big nasty hill and I'm sitting in the sand with fat bunched up knees and the beginning of a rash on my temple. I feel ugly. I'm slithering in my own murky filth and metallic blacked blood is drying like a rotten fruit beneath my fingernails. I want a shower, a boiling bath, soap, water, clean things. Get the alcohol

taste off my tongue. Get the oil and sweat off my skin. Make me clean. Please nasty questioning woman, make me clean again![2]

We hadn't read that then but we knew that psychologically you were in no state to hold down a job. We appealed to the Tribunal to reverse the Atos decision. They said you needed a full assessment from a psychiatrist before they would consider your appeal. Your GP explained to us that no way could he get a referral to a psychiatrist in a matter of weeks. You'd only get emergency psychological help if you did something really serious like jumping out of a window and breaking your leg. He was genuinely frustrated and upset about this state of affairs. He told us that we would have to go to a private psychiatrist, in order to get an assessment in time. He recommended one in Hove, the Priory Hospital. It would be expensive but necessary. So Dr Bowskill saw you. He had a short interview with you and looked at your notes. He very promptly sent a summary saying that you were not mentally fit for work. He went on to say that, in his opinion, you needed a further in-depth diagnosis and treatment.

The day of the Tribunal arrived. We came round to your flat in the morning. You were in a state of high anxiety. You said you'd had a terrible time last night with some young men who'd verbally and physically abused you. It sounded to us like a story you'd made up as an excuse not to come. But you were sitting on the bed, huddled up in a duvet, shivering and pale. I made mugs of tea, Amanda hugged you and gently tried to cajole you. The Tribunal needed to hear you and see you if they were to understand why you couldn't work and needed your benefit. Without it you would never be able to rent anywhere to live.

2　Excerpt from a short story 'What Happened to Your Face?' by Colette.

Landlords, at that time, only accepted unemployed tenants if they had guaranteed money coming in. Amanda got you dressed. We gently persuaded you down the stairs and into the car.

Your Tribunal consisted of a male doctor and a female solicitor. Given your state they allowed us to sit in. Early in the hearing the solicitor gently asked you how you were feeling. Instead of directly answering her, you blurted out a version of what you'd told us earlier.

'How do you think I feel? I was attacked last night by six men.'

'Oh really, what happened?' she asks calmly.

'It was at a filling station shop. They pulled me into their van and took me to my flat. Then they raped me.'

A silence while this sinks in. 'Have you reported this to the police?' the doctor asks.

'No point is there?' you respond, looking away distractedly.

Amanda and I could see the doctor look to the solicitor. It seemed they thought you were a very disturbed young woman. If so they were right. The decision took less than ten minutes. They recommended that not only should your benefit be reinstated but it should be increased. They said that you were not capable of work. They also recommended that you have further psychological help. We agreed, but where was it to come from?

Now that you would be able to pay rent, we were able to try and find you somewhere to live. Seven Dials is only a mile from where you had been living. The flat we found was pretty rundown. Even the estate agent admitted it was 'tired and in need of a bit of TLC'. But the rooms were big and you liked that. From our point of view the cooker and heating were all electric, there was no gas supply in the flat. That was a paramount safety issue. Your new landlord was okay about you being on benefit, knowing that his rent was guaranteed. It was the end of October – half term. So Chloe, Teddy and their two boys drove down and helped you into your new home. Teddy connected up your old TV, installed your little CD/radio player (music was always important to you). They ordered in takeaway pizzas for you all. Everyone tried to be optimistic about the move – another new beginning?

Dave was, at least temporarily, out of your life. He had been excluded from Brighton and was now in a hostel in Kent. The police case against him on five charges of assault and domestic violence, etc. was called for the Magistrate's Court on 23rd November. We got there and met your Crown Prosecution Service (CPS) solicitor. She was young and keen. She seemed to think that you had strong grounds for a prosecution. We waited while it was decided which courtroom the case would be heard in. Your anxiety levels went sky high. You were terrified at the thought of seeing Dave again. You were terrified of the lawyers you were to meet. You started to hyperventilate. We tried to calm you. A court liaison volunteer talked you through what was to come. Then, half an hour later, we were told the court had been double-booked and your case would not be heard today. It was to be postponed until the new year. The feeling of deflation was immense for all of us but for you it was a hammer blow. You'd been really strong. Your drinking was now under control. You'd bought some new clothes. You'd even started going to yoga classes. You were preparing yourself to face this confrontation with Dave. And now you were told it would be another eight weeks. How could you believe them? How could you deal with the next two months? We weren't sure that you could...

CHAPTER 18

The Law Is...

It's dark. No one will lift out a hand. They won't listen to me. I must take one day at a time, they said. But I can't. And do you know, I really cannot understand the language that you speak.[1]

When a woman has been physically assaulted and abused, reasonable people might expect that legal processes would protect her. When the police, and the CPS, have used their considerable powers of persuasion to get that woman to pursue her assailant in the courts, people might expect them to support that woman. They might also expect that the prosecuting solicitor would work closely with the vulnerable plaintiff to establish her case. That, as many female victims of violence and rape would testify to, is not the way our legal system works in practice.

A new year had dawned. All three of us stand outside the brutal concrete structure that is Brighton Magistrates' Court. We complete the security checks. Your case is to be called first thing. We arrive in the waiting room at 9.30 am. We are told your

---

1   From one of Col's diaries.

solicitor has been held up but will be with you shortly, to run through the day's proceedings. A couple of hours pass, by now you are getting extremely stressed. At approximately midday, a flustered looking, middle-aged woman comes hurrying in, clinging onto bulging files of papers. She asks if Colette McCulloch is here. You answer that you are and we add that we are your parents.

'Hello Colette, I'm your CPS solicitor,' she states while fumbling to open her bulging briefcase.

All three of us regard her in amazement. We've never seen her before.

'What happened to the solicitor who was here with us in November?'

'Not sure, think she's on another case. Sorry, can you give me a moment, only got all this, this morning. I'll go over it in my fifteen-minute lunch break.'

She starts to fumble through the wads of paper she's carried in. For a moment we are speechless. Amanda and I stare at her in disbelief. We struggle to contain our anger; we don't want to upset you any further.

Amanda reacts first:

'This is so unfair, so wrong. Col's waited a whole year for this court case.'

'And you expect to represent her after ten minutes reading it up,' I add in cold fury.

You look on saying nothing. Your face says it all. Worse is to follow in the court itself, as the hearing gets under way. Your new solicitor stumbles through the evidence against Dave. It is extensive. Dave eyeballs you from the dock. You don't know where to look. The police do not give evidence in person, their statements are read out. Dave has had the same legal aid solicitor for months now. He is well briefed. He starts to cross-examine you. The basis of his argument is that nobody can believe a word you say because his client states, there is evidence that you have mental health problems. Your solicitor objects to this line but the magistrates rule that the evidence should be heard. This seems totally unjust to you. Dave's criminal record cannot be mentioned in court. But your medical records are to be openly discussed and held against you. Thus when you are questioned about your mental health, you can contain yourself no longer:

'Me?! What about him and what he's done...?'

'Miss McCulloch, just answer the question!' comes the stern response from the bench.

'But he's been in prison twice for beating people up. Isn't that...'

'Silence! You will be excluded if you continue. Court will adjourn for fifteen minutes while you calm down.'

You rush out to the toilets and vomit. Your fears had been well founded. It was a real eye-opener for us as well. The defence solicitor was cold and brutal in his cross-examination. The whole hearing gave the appearance that it was you who was on trial, not your assailant.

Times stood still;
A moments hush.
A whisper that I barely heard.
A flickering madness,
The burning fear.
Cold sweat;
Bitter salt tear.
Oh my God,
What land is this
That promises no comfort?
What was it in this mind of mine

That made me act so shamelessly?
How did I let it come to this;
A wall and empty seats.
Shoot me; please!
Hold out your hand and carry me off
To mountains distant whispering.[2]

The opening lines of a poem you wrote years earlier. You had very similar feelings in the courthouse that day in January 2012.

It was hard to persuade you back in from the toilets when the court reconvened. How can it be that an abused young woman is not allowed to speak the truth while a violent man's impunity is protected by the law? No wonder women are reluctant to bring actions against men for domestic violence or indeed rape. We all felt the CPS had let you down badly. The whole process had taken over a year. We'd had one false start, two adjournments and three different CPS solicitors – the last of whom had only fifteen minutes to read up your case.

It was hard to tell what the opinion of the three magistrates was. For reasons I never understood, the police forensic photos of the bruises Dave had inflicted on you were never produced in court. The police never explained. As they didn't attend the hearing we weren't able to ask them. The case was adjourned till 29th February, when verdicts on the five charges would be given. In the meantime Dave must return to his hostel in Kent and have no contact with you. Dave was grinning as he left the court. He clearly didn't take the case seriously as he texted you later saying:

'That was a laugh. See you soon babe!'

Luckily, it wasn't necessary for you to attend the final hearing. You didn't want to, so Amanda stayed with you and I went

---

2   From 'Shoot Me Please' by Colette.

on my own. Dave was found guilty on only two counts out of the five. It was enough to ensure he would continue to be excluded from Brighton, put on probation and must not attempt to contact you in any way. You had changed your mobile number, so this time maybe he might be kept out of contact. The CPS seemed pleased. We felt Dave had largely got away with it and would still be a danger to other women in the future. You felt degraded and diminished by the whole process. You were exhausted. Your self-esteem was in shreds.

Meanwhile you finally got your referral to a psychiatrist. Amanda went with you to your first appointment with Dr B. He asked about your medical history. Which drugs you had been on for your OCD and anxiety. Whether you were allergic to any anti-depressants you'd been prescribed.

'Yes,' you said. 'Seroxat. I get double vision and I pull my hair out in my sleep. Mum had to talk to the doctors about it.'

'She's quite right, she had a bad allergic reaction. They took her off it,' Amanda added.

He noted all this down. Discussing your acute anxiety he suggested that medication was the only immediate solution. CBT (Cognitive Behavioural Therapy) wasn't available for at least a year. He prescribed a course of Paroxetine and made an appointment to see you again in two months. You agreed to try it. Four days later Amanda's phone goes.

'Mum...the meds. I'm pulling my hair out again. It's all over my pillow!'

Were you exaggerating? We knew you distrusted all medics and medicaments by this stage. However, Amanda got on a train and went down to see you. She saw your hair on the pillow and your distressed state. She took you to your GP. He asked what Dr B had prescribed for your anxiety. Amanda showed him the carton of Paroxetine. The GP looked at it and said, 'That's just the generic form of Seroxat, the same drug. Not surprising you're having the same side effects.'

You and your mum were incredulous – how could he do that? The GP took you off it and prescribed diazepam (Valium) to reduce your anxiety instead. This was a disastrous start with your new psychiatrist. Not surprisingly you lost all confidence in him. Dr B's attitude to you seemed to be that you were irresponsible and uncooperative. There was no discussion about the causes for your self-destructive behaviour. He told you that there could be no treatment for you, until you stopped drinking. He saw your alcohol abuse as wilful, rather than self-medication to blunt your chronic anxiety.

Throughout the year you attended the two local self-help groups. But they were mainly made up of women who'd had their babies taken into care. You didn't really fit in. We found a private therapist for you. You said you liked her but you would often miss your appointments. However, on a personal level, you did meet and form a relationship with a guy who lived nearby. He was in his thirties and single. He seemed to like you a lot, as you did him. In April 2012 you wrote to your old friend from the Bethlem days, Caroline (Caz) Spray, about the relationship:

> I am seeing a guy at the moment, but I'm a bit of a commitment phobe, so taking it a bit slowly; ie only meeting up once a week. He knows my problems + is v understanding.

Some weeks later, in a wide-ranging letter to Caz:

As for seeing Tim to help, it sort of does but once he has left I go mental!!! I do drink with Tim, but only wine, and my addiction is vodka because it knocks me out and stops me worrying and over-thinking.

Then further on in the same letter:

One of my probs, at the mo, is I get very nervous just before seeing Tim. I often OD on valium, so that's rather worrying. I just get self conscious + worried. I'm convinced I won't be able to smile, + go red etc. So I often put off seeing him. It's sad because I'm very fond of him.

We never met Tim (not his real name) but he sounded a decent and sensitive guy. But you found being with people you liked, and who cared for you, oppressive after a short time. Not only did you put off meeting them, you would often end the meeting abruptly. Whenever Amanda or I visited you, towards the end of the day you would suddenly say: 'You must go now, it's time for you to leave.' It was the same with Tim. You'd virtually push him out of your flat earlier than he expected. You found it incredibly hard to just be with someone, however fond of them you were.

I remember when we met.
I sat provocatively near you and your friends
In the bar near the station to no where.

And you said, after, that you had seen me and
    thought me beautiful
When I entered the room and it was strange
Because I had never thought I could be seen that way.

Having got him to leave, now facing the void of being on your own, you would 'go mental'. You would frequently drink vodka and self-harm. In the years of 2011 and 2012 you ended up in A&E 72 times, according to your GP's records. Sometimes, only hours after leaving your flat, Tim would receive a call from you saying you were in hospital again. It was too much for him. You had told us that he was something of a romantic. In his thirties, he had never lived with anyone. He found the responsibility of looking after you and your mood changes deeply unsettling. He'd leave you quite happy – two hours later you were in A&E. He couldn't live like that. He was becoming anxious himself. He said the relationship must finish. You told us that you'd thought he was going to ask you to live with him. Repeating patterns; you'd missed all the signals.

Do you remember what you said that night?
That when I asked you if you loved me, and you
Said you did not know
And I went mad,
You then said that you had loved the girl
Who entered the bar
Near the station to no where
But not the girl before you.
It hurt in as much as I went home bleeding
Thoughts I could never express.
And that I still think of you

As a person I could never deserve.
And that I listen to the CD you compiled for me
With Chemical Colette neatly margined in its side
Much the same as you would curl in upon my
    curledness.
I miss you.
I'm sorry.
I promise, when I have the heart to do so,
I will erase you from my mind.[3]

You came out to France for Christmas with us and Chloe and her family. (We'd signed the sales agreement but we hadn't yet completed the sale.) It was hard to believe that it was only three years since you'd spent Christmas here, with us all, and Jamie. Then everything had seemed possible: a good degree, a loving relationship with your man and a positive future together. As you faced another new year, we all knew that optimism had vanished.

---

3   From 'On You Saying No' by Colette.

CHAPTER 19

A Perfect Storm...

Selling a house in France can be a bureaucratic marathon. After eighteen months on the market we received an offer. Various surveys and checks had to be carried out. In September we signed the sales agreement. We completed end of January 2013. Our buyers didn't want to take possession until the autumn. So the deal was that we would take care of the house until then. So we could have a last summer holiday there, and turn our full attention onto life in the UK.

You had a strong constitution but stress and your chaotic lifestyle was affecting your physical health. Something that had long puzzled us was how accident prone you were. Over the years you'd broken two fingers, your nose, sprained your ankle and broken your left wrist. (This does not include the injuries inflicted on you by various abusive boyfriends over the years.) Another consequence of not yet knowing you were autistic was that we didn't realise that, as someone on the spectrum, you were more at risk of having physical accidents than neuro-typical adults. As a Danish study by Svend Erik Mouridsen and colleagues states:

A clinical cohort of 341 Danish individuals with variants of ASD (autistic spectrum disorder)...now on average 43 years of age,

were updated with respect to mortality and causes of death...
In all, 26 persons with ASD had died, whereas the expected
number of deaths was 13.5. Thus the mortality risk among those
with ASD was nearly twice that of the general population. The
Standard Mortality Rate was particularly high in females...[1]

Because you hadn't yet been identified as being on the spectrum,
none of your care had focused on these issues. It's worth noting
that the risks were seen to be 'particularly high in females' and
these mortalities were often caused through accidents.[2]

You'd had a metal plate put into a wrist broken in an accident
a few years earlier. Your GP said it now had to be removed.

With the increasing privatisation in the health service, this
was to be carried out at a private facility twenty-five miles away.
It would be a painful operation. The clinic was not reachable by
public transport. You don't drive so after care would be difficult.
Amanda stayed with you for several days post your discharge.
While you had asked her to be with you, you soon found that
her presence disrupted your routine. For instance you didn't
allow her to get up until you were showered and dressed. This
could take some time! You wouldn't allow her to go the loo, you
wouldn't allow her to make a cup of coffee. On the one morning
she did so, she put the coffee jar back on the wrong shelf. You
exploded and threw a chair across the room. There is no reason-
ing with OCD. It was time to leave. Next day you accidentally
banged your wrist. The stitches opened. Another trip into A&E.
Luckily it wasn't too serious.

Your life in Seven Dials was developing into an unhealthy

---

1   Mouridsen, S. E., Brønnum-Hansen, H., Rich, B. and Isager, T. (2008) 'Mortality
     and causes of death in autism spectrum disorders: An update.' *Autism* 12, 4,
     403–414.
2   *Ibid.*

pattern. As winter turned to spring, then to summer, your attendance at the self-help groups became sporadic. The only one you persevered with was Refuge, the charity providing support for women who've experienced domestic violence. They asked you to write about your experiences, which you duly did. On reading your words, they were so impressed, they asked if they could use them in their self-help literature. This was a huge boost to your self-esteem but you still remained isolated. You made no friends. We suggested you join a film club, a walkers' group, or drawing classes in order to socialise. None of this worked for you. In March you had a really unproductive meeting with your psychiatrist Dr B. It was decided that you should be referred on. Another waiting list. You tried some voluntary work in a charity shop but you soon gave up on it. You frequented the more down-market local pubs to seek out company. You took up with a series of less and less desirable men, over the months. Many were drug users. Most abused alcohol. They used you and your flat to 'party' in. Seven Dials is very central and your flat was in a convenient spot for these men to hang out. The front door of the building was often left on the latch by the young guys, who occupied the basement. Anyone passing by could get in. So anyone who knew you did just that. They climbed the stairs and bashed on your door, at all hours. You became very scared. We talked to your GP again about you having a social worker to support you, as you'd had in Wandsworth. He told us that, with the cutbacks, there were no social workers available for cases like yours.

Your new address, however, was coming to be known to the local police, as were you. Not surprising given the company you were keeping. You were soon on first name terms with a number of cops. You would be walking down the street, with Amanda,

past a squad car waiting at the lights. You would wave at one of
the cops.

'Hey Terry, who're you arresting this time then?' you grin
cheekily.

The young, good-looking cop turns, and smiles at you.

'Behave yourself Colette…you take care.'

With that the squad car revs and pulls away. Amanda looks
at you in surprise.

'You know that policeman, love?'

'There was a punch up in the pub. Cops were called. Terry
arrested the bloke I was with.'

'What…?'

'Gave me a lift back afterwards. Fit, isn't he Ma?' you laugh.

You still relished shocking your parents with your behaviour.
In truth what shocked us was the way you were gravitating to
real lowlife guys on the criminal fringes. You'd laugh about how
you got barred from pubs and clubs with them. What you didn't
tell us was how they were taking all your benefit money off you.
You related how Terry and other cops reasoned with you about
your behaviour.

'You're an intelligent young woman, Colette…educated. What
are you doing with these guys? They'll just drag you down.'

You couldn't listen to anyone – the police, your GP, the
self-help groups or us. It was as though you were hell-bent on
self-destruction. Then out of the blue you'd call and tell us you'd
thrown all the booze away. You were going to the hairdressers,
to have a cut and re-style, then onto Waterstones to buy some
books. You could stay dry for weeks. But it never lasted.

8th July 2013 I phoned you and arranged to meet the next
day at your flat. Your finances were in a mess and direct debits
were being refused, as was your card at the ATM. You'd never
had much idea about money and you were getting worse. Your

so-called mates were stealing from you. We needed to sort something out with the bank. The idea was for you to have two accounts. One account which your benefit was paid into. Your rent and bills were paid from this by direct debit. You weren't able to touch this account, you had no cheque book or bank card for it. From this account a weekly allowance would be paid into the second account. This was your spending account with cheque book and bank card. The money was for living: food, clothes, travel, etc. If you overspent on this you would have to wait till the end of the week. You agreed in principle and were quite happy about it. It would stop the dodgy guys taking you to the ATM and emptying your account.

Before catching the train down, I called you to check you were still okay to meet me. I got no answer from your mobile. On several occasions one of us had made the journey down, only for you to refuse to see us. I didn't fancy a wasted journey and considered postponing my trip. I called Amanda, who was out of London, and she persuaded me to go.

'She was probably up late, just sleeping in. You must go. Got to stop them taking her money.' Amanda was quite right.

I walk up the hill from Brighton Station past the faded elegance of the stucco houses. Overweight seagulls swoop and squawk overhead. A homeless guy lies in a sleeping bag in a derelict shop doorway. A potent reminder of how threadbare support is for anyone vulnerable. I ring your doorbell. No answer. *Déjà vu.* Was it only two years ago that I'd stood outside your previous flat getting no answer? I'd called the police then but this time we'd made copies of your keys in case of emergencies.

Your flat is at the top of the rundown house. I knock on your door. Nothing. I call your mobile. I can hear it ringing in the flat. I gently open the door and call out your name. Nothing. There is a short staircase from the door up into the flat itself.

There's a bedroom to the left and a sitting room to the right and the kitchenette straight ahead. I call your name again. No answer. I turn right, push open the living room door and look in. On the table are greasy plates with half-eaten food, mugs full of ash and incongruously your open laptop. The grubby carpet is littered with takeaway packaging, empty lager cans, wine and vodka bottles. Amidst the debris the shape of a still body. You're lying on your back on the floor. You aren't moving.

I kneel down and touch your cheek. There is a red graze on your forehead. How long have you been lying here? Your skin feels ice cold. I search for a pulse in your neck. It's faint but there. I call 999. The guy is brilliant; asks all the right questions, keeps me calm talking till the paramedics arrive. A man and a woman; they reassure me. I sense my daughter's in safe hands. They check you out and change your wet clothes. Still unconscious you're put on a stretcher and taken out to the ambulance. The paramedics are fantastic. I travel with you to the hospital. A&E is like a disturbing sequence in a low budget apocalypse movie. Corridors jammed with trolleys bearing the injured with smashed limbs and gashed faces, or the frightened elderly, who have little idea where they are. Overworked nurses and doctors are just about coping.

A tube is inserted up your nose and fluid pumped into your stomach. You are very dehydrated. Blood samples are taken, drips set up. The exhausted female junior doctor says you're lucky to be alive. Still unconscious you're taken to a short-stay ward. I sit with you. The hours pass. It is evening. I must have nodded off. I wake to see you looking to me with cool eyes.

'Why'd you bother, Dad?'

'What do you mean?'

'It's obvious... No more grief for you and Mum, end of.'

It's a thump to the gut. All the air is knocked out of me.

'Don't Col... Don't ever think like that, don't ever say that.'

For a moment we are both still. I lean forward and hug you, through the tangle of tubes that you're attached to. We both cry as we hold each other. You soon drift off to sleep again. I tell the nurse I have to get some food. I call our friends Caroline and Edmond and ask if I can stay the night. They, as ever, welcome me. Caroline says she will visit you while I obtain some emergency medication for my glaucoma – I hadn't anticipated staying the night. Caroline is a warm human being and an ex teacher, who takes no prisoners. She marches up to your bed in the ward and says: 'Well now Col, who's been a silly girl?' You like Caroline; she makes you laugh. You were discharged the next morning.

It is now October, we have moved back to the UK and you have been in and out of A&E many times in the last few months. Now you have a new obsession. Every month you become convinced that you are pregnant. We've always advised you strongly against having unprotected sex. You still wouldn't take the contraceptive pill, though you often took the morning after pill, which messed up your metabolism. You had, to a large extent, ignored our advice but over the years you hadn't fallen pregnant. We had begun to think, with all your years of not eating interrupting your menstrual cycle, that maybe it was unlikely to happen.

But recently you've been having a relationship with a much younger guy, around twenty-three. He is hooked on heroin. You met him in A&E. He already has a child who he has no contact with. We advise that you should have nothing to do with him. He's clearly disturbed, with a lot of problems. Once again, as though testing the boundaries of how far you can go, you ignore our advice. For the last few months you have been buying pregnancy kits only to find that you are not pregnant. It seems that you want to be. In mid-October you go to your GP and have a test – it's negative. But you are convinced he's wrong. You go back two weeks later and see another, female GP. She tells you what you want to know and in truth are terrified of – you are pregnant!

The news is overwhelming for you, and creates the most appalling dilemma for us, and all who are trying to care for you.

Pale self-portrait sketch

CHAPTER 20

A Hard Place...

I'm learning something every passing day that the past is a place to hide when the future is too scary. Too scary even to contemplate, let alone set out upon.[1]

'Colette if you decide to go through with this, as doctors, our priority has to be to protect the unborn baby. You'd have to cut out all alcohol, smoking and drugs. You'd have to eat three meals every day. The father's a heroin addict. He won't help you. You'd have to change your life totally.'

She was the third doctor you'd consulted at your GP practice since the pregnancy had been confirmed. All three gave the same advice. It was a good caring practice. You'd been a patient there for three years. They knew you well. They had records of all your admissions to A&E. Much of your suicidal ideation, self-harm, alcohol abuse, the domestic abuse you suffered and your depression. Though, like us, they knew nothing of your autism at this stage. They had been unable to get you sufficient psychological support but they were aware of how delicate your mental health

---

was. They knew there was almost no chance of you being able to cope with a full-term pregnancy and birth. They had to leave the decision to you, but the doctors were in close touch with us and let us know how concerned they were.

We spent days walking round Brighton and talking with you throughout these GP meetings. You wanted your mum to be there with you for the consultations, but not to speak unless you asked her to. We were torn as to what should be done. If the pregnancy went ahead, we knew that as you put on weight, you'd panic. The shadow of anorexia still stalked you. The looming reality of your body becoming out of control, getting bigger and bigger, scared you. The female GP understood this. She patiently explained that in the years they'd known you, you hadn't been able to change your ways. If you didn't there was no way you'd be allowed to keep the baby. Your young heroin-addict boyfriend wanted no part of this and had distanced himself. We were in our seventies... There was no easy solution.

You were wracked with indecision. You were overwhelmed by all the information. In the end it was fear – fear of all the changes that would take over your life that made you opt for termination.

Only six weeks pregnant, you went ahead with the procedure. Amanda went with you and stayed with you afterwards for a week. Your moods veered from relief that it was over, to emotional regret. But your reaction was less extreme than we'd feared. And one good thing did come out of this crisis. In December you were finally given an appointment with a highly qualified psychiatrist.

Dr Pannu is consultant psychiatrist and Clinical Director of Brighton and Hove Care Delivery Service. He asked us to come to your first appointment with him. He had traced all your medical notes going back to when you were at school. He'd gone through your whole history by the time we met. He was the first clinician to do this since Janet Treasure. We were impressed. At the end of the consultation he diagnosed that your anxiety was caused by a mental illness called Borderline Personality Disorder. Dr Pannu explained that it was a condition that young women with eating disorders often suffered from. He was confident that the effects could be alleviated with a combination of medication and CBT (Cognitive Behavioural Therapy). He took on-board your experience with Seroxat. He prescribed fluoxetine (Prozac) to calm you down. He'd read, in your notes, that you'd taken it before with no ill effects. Then after eight weeks or so you would begin a course of CBT. You were to wait till after Christmas, start the Prozac then come back to see him in early February. You'd have to cut back your drinking or it would negate any benefit. While we hadn't even heard of Borderline Personality Disorder, it did seem that we were finally getting somewhere. You said you were willing to try the treatment.

You came to stay with us for our first Christmas in our new south-east London home. The house is small. You liked it. You were particularly taken with it having a shed in the garden. With a twinkle in your eye, you suggested, 'One day I'll take over this house and you Mum will be banished to the studio shed. I'll feed you bits of bread and chicken legs through the window bars. Like Hansel and Gretel.'

You thought this was hysterical. Your dark sense of humour was definitely returning.

Of course we spent some evenings going over what had happened with the pregnancy. At times you blamed us. At other times you accepted that the decision was probably the right one. We also discussed Dr Pannu's diagnosis and your taking medication again. All in all it was an emotional time. Christmas can be tough for anyone with mental health problems. It is littered with potential meltdowns. We had a few, but lots of hugs and love as well. Somehow we navigated our way onto the dry land of the new year. On 2nd January 2014 I took you back to Brighton by train. Travelling alone always made you anxious.

Charcoal drawing of Amanda

The first few weeks on Prozac went well. You took the prescribed amount. You started a portraiture class. We kept in close touch on the phone and by visiting. You were calmer. You were happier. It was the best we'd seen you look in ages. But after four weeks, you got lonely and bored. You started to revisit your old haunts with the dodgy guys you'd hung out with. Amanda visited you at the beginning of February and you walked to a café together. Suddenly you lurched into the road. Amanda just managed to pull you back from the path of a fast-moving car. Angry horns were sounded. It turned out you had taken ketamine. A few days later, you lost your keys, your bank card and your bag. Once again your life was becoming a roller coaster.

On 6th February 2014 we had an appointment with Dr Pannu to review the position. His feeling was that while you'd lapsed a couple of times you were making progress. CBT would only work if you were totally committed to it. We left the meeting with you saying you were determined to complete the treatment. But, as ever, what you said and what you could do were very different things. You were soon missing out on the Prozac. This was disappointing. Unless it is taken regularly it does more harm than good. Dr Pannu stopped prescribing it to you.

He did, however, achieve one of the priorities we'd been asking for over the years – getting you a social worker as your care co-ordinator. You met Liz Hennessy in early spring. She is an empathetic, caring social worker in her forties. She was to establish an important and strong relationship with you. She attempted to get your life on a more even keel. By now the low life you hung out with were often in your flat. There were fights. In April one of them broke your nose. Once again you were back in A&E.

You were getting through money fast. The bank was letting you run up a big debt. You'd found a way round the safety net we'd put in place and were now accessing your direct debit account, meant only for rent and bills. This was still what they called a student account and allowed for an overdraft up to £1,500. At this point your debt was £1,000. We decided to ask the bank to freeze your overdraft at that level. You were no longer a student and were not able to work. Your bank branch was in London, the same one as Amanda's. She went in to see the bank manager there. She explained our proposition. He refused saying we'd need a court injunction to limit the overdraft. Amanda responded, 'This is totally wrong. You're allowing my daughter's overdraft to increase when she's living on benefit. That's crazy.'

'It's her bank account. She's an adult. Without an injunction you have no authority.'

'She has four mental health diagnoses. She can't work. There is no way she can ever pay this off. And then you will charge her interest. That's immoral.'

'Sorry madam, but that's the situation.'

The bank continued to lend you money up to your limit of £1,500. There was an ironic corollary to this. Days after you died, when we were closing down your accounts at the bank, the 'bereavement manager' asked if we would like to pay off your overdraft? There was a long hard pause.

'I think not,' said Amanda through gritted teeth.

Your so-called friends eventually sussed you had access to easy money. They would come round and demand cash, claiming you owed them for drugs they'd supplied. They would take you down to the ATM and get you to empty your account. Once we realised what was going on, I went to see you. While we talked, a drunken young guy rang the doorbell and shouted up to you. I went down and refused to let him in. He threatened me and went on shouting. I called the police. They arrested him and took him away. But of course they let him go a few hours later.

Liz was trying to organise support for you. A care assistant, Mary, was detailed to see you once a fortnight. Some weeks later we arrange to meet you, Liz and Mary at your flat. We all five sit in the living room and discuss how to make your life safer. After a few minutes Mary glances to the door, having heard something.

'Colette, is there anyone else in the flat?'

You shake your head.

'Are you sure Colette?' You look away, guiltily. Mary, a slight woman in her forties, smartly gets up, leaves the room, crosses the landing and flings open your bedroom door.

'Right you two, out of here. Out!'

In the bedroom, two large young men stumble around trying to gather up their clothes and shoes. One is the guy who had threatened me, the other one I don't know. But Mary knows them both...

'Leave it out! We're doing nothing!' one of them mumbles.

'I said get out of here! And I mean NOW!!' she commands loudly.

The shamefaced pair scurry away down the stairs and out. Liz and Mary turn to you.

'I did say they could sleep here, they'd been out all night,' you protest, quite enjoying the scene.

'As we were saying Colette, those two are known addicts and dealers. You don't seem to understand. You must keep them out or we can't keep you safe.'

Living as you were, there was little chance of that though. The landlord was beginning to make threats of eviction. Mary was to spend a lot of time with you. She took you to coffee bars, vintage clothes shops and walks by the sea. You enjoyed her company but once she was gone, your anxieties would return. We all realised that you couldn't continue to live like this.

Meanwhile, Liz had arranged for a clinical psychologist and a specialist nurse practitioner to look into your case. A meeting was set up for you and us to see them. You missed the meeting but Rebecca Simpson, the nurse practitioner, said that she suspected that you might be autistic. Amanda and I were sceptical, to say the least. I have a nephew who has been diagnosed as being Asperger's. He is a bright guy but also has classic autistic traits. Throughout his childhood he couldn't look people in the eye. He couldn't speak to people, unless he knew them well. He didn't make friends. He was gluten intolerant with digestive problems.

He hated being touched and was chronically shy. You showed none of these traits. You could talk for Britain, you were often noisy, you were 'touchy feely'. You looked people in the eye. We couldn't see how you could have the same condition.

Rebecca was very interested that you had a cousin who was Asperger's. She said she'd like to carry out a series of diagnostic observations. We were unconvinced, as was Dr Pannu when we discussed it with him. Meanwhile you were facing another eviction. There'd been more complaints about noise from your flat. The estate agent delivered an ultimatum: the rows and fights must stop or your lease would be terminated and you'd be out.

In August Rebecca asked you to bring us to a meeting at the Polyclinic in Hove. She explained to us your condition, which she said was High Functioning Autistic Spectrum Disorder. What used to be called Asperger's Syndrome. The same condition as my nephew had. We were perplexed. She went on to explain how autism in women presented very differently from men. She said you, like many women, masked your condition. Laura James states:

> Copying neurotypical behaviour is an exceptionally strong coping mechanism in most autistic girls.[2]

She goes on to quote Professor Tony Attwood:

> In terms of how girls react, I think one of the common ways is to observe, analyse and imitate and create a mask, which delays diagnosis for decades until the wheels fall off.[3]

---

2   James, L. (2018) *Odd Girl Out: My Extraordinary Autistic Life*. Berkeley, CA: Seal Press.

3   Attwood, T. (2007) *The Complete Guide to Asperger's Syndrome*. London: Jessica Kingsley Publishers.

Rebecca went on to outline how your anxiety, your obsessions, your creativity were all part of this condition. She asked if she could look at some of your writing and art, before writing up your Complex Case Review. You agreed. Amanda had kept most of your drawings, paintings and poems from the age of five and would get them to her. Meanwhile Liz was looking for somewhere more suitable for you to live. They realised that you needed specialist care for your autism and couldn't live alone. You had a lot of problems but at least now, *at the age of thirty-three*, you had a diagnosis – High Functioning Autistic Spectrum Disorder.

After Rebecca's explanation and much further reading, the diagnosis began to make sense to us. Above all it explained why you repeated such self-destructive behaviours and how you never understood that actions have consequences. It explained your obsessions right back to watching *The Wizard of Oz* over and over again, aged three. Only later did we learn that autism and anorexia are connected. There have also been a number of papers explaining connections between the conditions of dyslexia and autism. Gradually the puzzle of your last thirty years began to fall into place for us.

You initially accepted the diagnosis but you never liked it. You hated terms like dyslexic, OCD, anorexic and the rest. Autism was just another label you reasoned. If they were wrong about Borderline Personality Disorder (BPD), why should you accept that they were right about this? In truth, autism is often mistaken for BPD, but that cut no ice with you. You were being labelled and you didn't like it. For you, autistic meant stupid and weird, like being back at school. You anticipated being controlled again by people who thought they knew you better than you did yourself. Your knee-jerk reaction to medics was total distrust.

Somehow, I must efface the memory of feeling. I must let go the senses, and cast them to the wind,
I must feel nothing.
I must become nothing
My obsessions will gradually fall to the wayside, because there is nothing left to do anything for.
Bit by bit, I will disintegrate. Become a part of the long silence in the sweep of a sofa's length. Everything I do will be imaginary; therefore of no importance.
Everything I've done has been thought through eagerly and intensely; like planning to be calm. Now, I will practice the art of being someone else. Become someone else. I will eavesdrop on conversations disinterestedly. I will become fourth wall to this room
I will not see, and I will not be seen.
I will stop speaking. Silence will become my speech
Bit by bit, I will become completely numb.
I will no longer miss the sound of birdsong. The wet trickle of rain down my neck. I will no longer pine the evenings, huddled by the fire to keep warm, being held in my mother's comforting embrace.
No longer will I reflect with bitter twisted 'knowledge' the errors of my ways and all it has cost me. I will become indifferent to everything; to where I am, to my age-old fears. Value will diminish. Existence no longer a throb in the breast.
Bit by intricate bit, I will become wholly numb.[4]

---

4   From 'The Numbing Game' by Colette.

This was one of the pieces of writing that Rebecca read and referred to in her Complex Case Review. I think it describes your autistic mind while trying to deny it. The diagnosis was to be a turning point, but with consequences none of us had envisaged.

CHAPTER 21

What Land Is This?

I know for sure my sleep is broken
Fragmented like my thoughts.
Unpredictable like my mind.
I'm reaching for something; an apple; a pear.
I don't know what.
But every move I make is hindered.
Stopped short by some accident of nature.
Wind. Uninvited seagulls. Thunderous skies.
I can never get there.[1]

Dr Pannu took time to research the subject of autism (autism in women was, and is still, not widely understood) and then agreed with Rebecca Simpson's conclusions. He pointed out that Borderline Personality Disorder and ASD have many symptoms in common, hence the wrong diagnosis. We were also in agreement. You continued to question the analysis, of course you did, you hated any label. The question now was what provision could be made for you?

Your landlord had had enough. You were to be evicted. The

---

1   Poem from one of Col's diaries.

medics realised that you needed to be in specialist, supported accommodation given your condition. There was no way you could live in a flat on your own again; it was too dangerous. And you were unable to share a flat with other people. Ever since you left the Maudsley, twelve years earlier, medics had said you needed to be in supported living. Janet Treasure had said it, Wandsworth Adult Social Care had said it, the university counsellor had said it. Now Sussex Partnership NHS Foundation Trust was saying it.

Liz Hennessy was searching for a suitable placement, for someone with your complex needs, but there seemed to be almost nothing available.

Shore House was once a fine substantial house set in a 19th-century terrace overlooking the sea and the Brighton front to the east of the pier. In autumn of 2014 its days of grandeur had clearly passed. It is described on its website as follows:

> Shore House is an innovative and dynamic service which provides accommodation and 24-hour intensive support to 20 people with a range of mental health diagnoses, and to those experiencing the effects of complex trauma.[2]

In reality, when we helped you move in, it turned out to be a large, ramshackle house with a shabby, crumbling interior and exterior. The men and women living there did indeed have a variety of mental health and substance misuse issues. Technically no drugs were allowed on the premises. You told us that in your experience this rule was frequently broken. Staff were well meaning but did not have much training or expertise in many mental health conditions, certainly not autism. It was not

---

2   Brighton Housing Trust (2019) *Shore House*. Accessed on 23/06/2020 at www. bht.org.uk/services/mental-health-wellbeing/shore-house.

even mentioned. The best we could hope for was that they would keep you safe until an appropriate placement could be found. Meantime it was the only accommodation available.

Shore House was a short-term solution with limited support. There were 'house meetings' each week where rules and behaviour were discussed. One-to-one sessions with staff could be arranged. But for you the counselling wasn't relevant to your condition. You needed a definite structure.

You continued to have contact with your old acquaintances. You spent as much time away from Shore House as you could.

> I can't go on like this I can't even get any privacy.
> Where does the brain go when it
> Cannot flee from itself?
> Where does the heart search when
> All places to love have been lost?[3]

There was one of your old friends, Charley (not his real name), that you continued to seek out. Charley was a heroin addict and one of the guys Mary threw out of your flat that time when we were there. He was a sad but devious mess. He lived in a council-owned flat, on benefit. He was overweight, in poor health and had Hepatitis C. You knew this. You had always been frightened of needles and injecting. You'd never dared to take heroin. But one night, round at his place, he persuaded you to try it. He injected you with a needle he'd already used.

Why did you let him do it? Was it just the impulse of the moment? Or was it yet another example of you wanting to test every boundary to its limits, never mind the danger? Whatever the reason, you phoned us the next morning in a complete panic.

---

3   Untitled poem in Col's autobiography.

You were terrified that you now had Hep C. You went straight to the sexual health clinic, at the hospital. You had a history of going there for reassurance that you hadn't caught a venereal disease after a casual sexual encounter. The results had always been negative, giving you the all-clear. And so it was this time. However, they said that you better come in for a follow-up test a few days later, as it might not show yet. They were right. Amanda went with you a week later. You tested positive. You were hysterical and in danger of having a total meltdown. They advised you to contact the haematology department at the hospital. Amanda talked you down and tried to reassure you.

We researched the illness online; Hepatitis C can be cured. Treatment doesn't start immediately as it is quite possible that the body will fight off the virus, provided you're leading a healthy lifestyle. Amanda arranged an appointment with the haematology department. The treatment available at that time was a long course of medication, with serious side effects for people with mental health problems. Clearly not suitable for you. A new American medication, which involves taking anti-viral tablets for only a matter of weeks, was not yet available in the UK. It was due to be taken up by the NHS the following year. The haematology unit recommended that you should wait for the American drug. It would be better anyway if you didn't take it until you were in a safer, more supportive environment than Shore House. Your short-term stay there, however, turned out not to be short – it continued for fifteen months.

I'm so-o-o bored. I'm so-o-o sick of this life. I so-o-o don't know how to change it.

Despite Liz's efforts no appropriate placement was found. This was deeply frustrating for you. You phoned us constantly.

'I can't stand it here! I want to come and stay with you.'

Which you did quite often. But being with us never answered your real problems. It only took a day or two before there was a huge row. It could be brought on by any number of things, big or small, but it always ended up with you shouting, 'I can't be with you two! Don't tell me what to do! I need my space! I'm going back to Brighton!'

With that you'd storm out of the house on a walk and get lost. You never had any sense of direction and you didn't know south-east London. A panic phone call would come two hours later. We'd rush out and try to find you, just like we had all those years ago when you walked out of our house in Putney. The difference was that now, the day after, you would get on a train back to Brighton. But wherever you went, your condition went with you. Could you ever escape your demons?

Meanwhile, you'd developed a relationship with another resident at Shore House who was a schizophrenic. He heard voices from God. He was essentially a gentle guy but when confused, he became violent. The two of you had some terrible bust-ups. After one he smashed up his room. The staff had him moved to another hostel nearby. This meant that you would go missing, and stay with him in his tiny room there. It was very bad for both of you. You made no other friends. Once again you could only relate to one person at a time. When you eventually left Shore House, they gave you a form to fill in commenting on your experience there. You added a long comment ending with:

I cannot lie, for I would not be doing you a service in doing so. I have left 'Shore House' marginally better equipped than when I came in. But it's like putting a plaster on a gaping wound. Happy with Shore House? Sorry No!

In fact you weren't better equipped at all when you left. It was no fault of Shore House but it had been fifteen wasted months. It was not the right place for someone with your complex needs. Meanwhile Liz had at last identified two possible placements. Without seeing you, the first said that they could not take you. That left only one possibility. It was at that time called Milton Park Therapeutic Campus run by a company called Brookdale Care...

CHAPTER 22

Milton Park

The Station to Nowhere

I have this dream that no one can hear me. That my mouth moves to the rhythm of my words, but no sound issues. When I open my mouth to speak they turn their backs. Walk away.[1]

Sussex Partnership Trust said that it was essential you had specialist inpatient care. Milton Park was the only clinic/care home offering such a placement that they could find. The modern buildings are fifty miles from London, halfway between Bedford and Cambridge. A short walk from the campus is the A1 dual carriageway. Heavy lorries thunder up and down this main artery to the North and Scotland. Since your death they have renamed Milton Park. It's now called Lakeside. A PR man's soothing name for a mental health unit situated just half a mile from one of the busiest roads in the UK, with not a lake in sight. That would've made you laugh, given how you hated the place. Likewise, three different limited companies have run the campus since you

---

1   From one of Col's diaries.

were there. Brookdale Care was taken over by the alarmingly named Tracscare, which some months later transitioned into Accomplish. A glance at the Companies House website to look up these three companies does not inspire confidence. In the last four years fifteen out of eighteen directors have resigned. Every time I check on the 'Lakeside' website the staff seem to have left and been replaced. Some posts changing several times. It is only three years since you were there and I can see almost no staff members who were there with you. Whatever name the place has, or whichever for-profit setup owns it, the mission statement below rings hollow. The glossy brochures and flashy websites that declare these words were, in our experience, totally misleading.

Milton Park employs an experienced clinical and therapeutic team of Consultant Psychiatrists, Psychologists, Speech & Language Therapists, Occupational Therapists and Specialist Nurses.

'One size fits all' doesn't work for those who live with Autism, Learning Disabilities or Mental Health Issues, this is why Brookdale offer a truly person-centred approach.[2]

We took the train to St Neots to visit Milton Park Campus on the 12th November 2015. Liz Hennessy brought you up in a car from Shore House, Brighton, a drive of 100 miles plus. We were all shown round together by the assistant manager Shaun Francis. You'd already been assessed by Gerry Graham, the general manager, earlier in the month. He'd come down and interviewed you at Shore House. He'd read the Complex Case Review carried out by Rebecca Simpson and Dr Howard for Sussex Partnership Trust. This document was the definitive assessment of your condition. Little notice was taken of it during your subsequent

---

2   Brookdale Care, Milton Park Brochure.

treatment at Milton Park, but it was to become a vital issue in the wake of your death. The result of Mr Graham's assessment was that, he said, they could treat you and supply the care your condition required. Shaun Francis told us that the best plan would be for you to have a ten-day close observation period in a secure ward. This would be useful for 'in-depth psychological input'. You would then move on to Pathway House, the open ward for high functioning residents. He went on to say that someone like you hardly needed the observation period but it would be helpful.

Shaun took us to Ashwood, a locked ward for women, in what they call the hospital. (I say 'call' because there were no medical facilities there, not even a proper first aid kit, it turned out.) There was the sound of angry raised voices. Some sort of crisis was taking place, so he hurried us on to Elstow Ward. This was quieter and smaller and also locked. He didn't linger, saying it was where your short observation period would take place. He then moved us on to Pathway House, a hundred yards away across the courtyard. This was where you would be for most of your stay. It was a light modern building. The feeling in it was calm. There were only twelve residents, split between two wards. Everyone had their own room. There were restrictions but with permission people were free to come and go. Shaun said that there was yoga, a gymnasium, art therapy and plenty of other activities available on the campus. Support staff would be on hand to help residents get out into the community and find voluntary work nearby. As Gerry Graham quotes in the brochure:

> We really see our job as supporting people into the community and giving them the skills to be successful there.[3]

---

3   Milton Park Brochure.

The medium-term plan would be for you to establish a routine of group therapy leading on to voluntary work. Then, after some months, move on to supported housing, also run by Brookdale Care, possibly in London. We all, including you, felt that Pathway House was the right place for you. We left the campus agreeing that this could be a genuine new beginning, enabling you to live a more stable life.

Liz had secured funding for the placement. Sussex Partnership Trust green-lit it and dates were arranged. You wanted to have Christmas with us in London and then go in. That made sense but it meant we would have to take you there, as nobody at Sussex would be available over the holiday period. We felt this gave you the wrong message; that *we* were placing you there rather than Sussex, but there was no other option. We helped you move out of Shore House before Christmas. As ever you found the change very disturbing. This time you were going to a clinic/care home you'd only seen once, in a part of the world you didn't know at all.

Christmas was not easy. Hardly surprising. Your admission date was 29th December. Life in our house became increasingly fraught and tense, as the date approached. Rows would erupt from nowhere. One moment you would be railing at us about your boyfriend in Brighton, saying that you never wanted to see him again. Then you would be phoning him and saying you wanted to go back to him. Whatever food Amanda cooked was wrong. I was a control freak because I discouraged your drinking. You would storm off and disappear. Then a panic phone call. You were lost. It was a very tense few days. I booked a rental car for the drive up to Milton Park. The evening before you said you wouldn't go there. We sat up half the night discussing this with you. If you didn't take this place you had run out of care options. There was no other choice – you must give it a go. Eventually, exhausted, you agreed and we all went to bed. But by the morning, panic had overtaken you. You had squirreled away some vodka, drunk it and changed your mind again. I called West Hub (the Adult Community Mental Health Team). They talked you down and we set off. It was a difficult journey. You were drunk. Your mood swung wildly between anger, panic and acceptance, then back again. You tried twice to get out of the moving car, in the midst of London traffic. It was incredibly dangerous. On arrival, admission to the ward went badly. Many staff were on Christmas holidays. All in all it was a disorganised and upsetting beginning. However, there was worse to come...

> We want individuals to gain an understanding of their diagnosis to develop coping strategies and learn how to manage their anxieties.[4]

Your mum kept a detailed, day-by-day diary throughout your stay at Milton Park. She was very concerned at your distress and the lack of treatment you were receiving. She felt a need to keep track of events as your stay there seemed to be spiralling out of control. Tragically she was proved absolutely right. We later used her diary to put down a chronology of what took place leading to your death. You were initially admitted to Ashwood, the locked ward, in the hospital at Milton Park. It was full of disturbed women, shouting and screaming. I put down a chronology from Amanda's diary. An excerpt from this chronology is below:

> **Friday 1st January:** Due to Colette's huge distress and our phone calls they agreed to move her down the corridor to the quieter Elstow Ward. She was *the only voluntary patient*. She still found

---

4   Milton Park Brochure.

the environment very frightening as some of the patients were extremely disturbed. The room she was allocated had no heating, a broken shower and a faulty electric plug. It took several days to sort these problems out.

Sunday 3rd January: Colette told us that she couldn't sleep because the woman next door kept banging on her door and shouting. 'I can't do this' she said. We told her to put her complaints in writing to Barry Hannon her psychologist. Andy also emailed this information through to Barry.

Wednesday 6th January: There was meeting with Barry, nursing staff and the doctors. They considered her request to move to Pathway. But she had to have an assessment first and then there would be lots of paperwork. This surprised us since Shaun had said she could have gone straight to Pathway on admission.

During this first week Colette developed a nasty rash on her forehead that turned out to be ringworm. It took six days before a doctor came to see her and another five days before her prescription arrived. And this is called a hospital?

Thursday 7th January: Andy emailed Liz Hennessy with his concerns about Colette's treatment. She replied that she would call Gerry Graham, general manager of Milton Park. Dr Oluwatayo visited Colette to tell her that the team agreed that she should move onto Pathway but she still needed an assessment.

Friday 8th January: She had her first session with psychologist Barry Hannon; ten days after her admission.

Monday 11th January: Andy and Amanda visited Colette in Elstow Ward. She was very unhappy. We had a meeting with chief nurse Dominique which was not very helpful.

Tuesday 12th January: The panel doctors said Colette's behaviour was exemplary and she could move onto Pathway. Barry said he would inform Fiona Joyner (head of Pathway) to carry out her assessment as soon as possible.

Monday 18th January: Colette is told there is no room available for her at Pathway for the moment. She was extremely upset.

Wednesday 20th January: Amanda visited Colette taking warm clothes, books and food for her. Her spirits were very low, she had no energy and was very pale. *She'd lost a lot of weight. When she first arrived she existed on black coffee and diet coke for six days. Nobody noticed she wasn't eating.*

> Many women live with additional conditions such as Eating disorders... Staff have an extensive understanding of these conditions and know how to develop care plans that support the whole person.[5]

Friday 22nd January: She has her assessment with Fiona at Pathway. She is told that she can have a place there but not for another four weeks! She had already waited nearly four weeks in the locked ward and now she faces a further four weeks.

Wednesday 27th January: She is finally granted an unescorted walk of one hour a day. She has to be body searched and blood tested every time on her return. If staff are busy she would be kept waiting outside in the cold for up to 15 minutes.

You'd been told you would be in a locked ward for a week or so. It ended up being seven weeks. You were High Functioning ASD; no understanding had been shown about your particular condition.

---

5   Milton Park Brochure.

Peace in a capsule; that's all I want. A moment out of time. A space between the pull and tug of now and yesterday.[6]

They knew very well that you had a history of eating disorders; no attention was paid to it. When under stress it was a behaviour you resorted to. No attempt was made to treat you differently let alone 'develop a care plan that supports the whole person'. You wrote to your friend Caroline Spray, from the Maudsley Eating Disorder days, about your time in Elstow Ward while you were there:

Dear Caz,

... Every day is a trial. I cannot be helped in the areas I require (my OCD type repetitive 'checking' my 'intrusive' thought patterns, etc, all of which date back to early childhood) because a lot of patients here require much more immediate attention... I have aspirations for the future; things I would like to achieve and experience. Voluntary work and, dare I say it, paid employment. I don't want to spend my days in an institution watching 'Jeremy Kyle' feeling like the only thing I have to look forward to is a walk (albeit 1 hr in the community) and countless fags and black coffees. Where it's even next to impossible to have my eczema cream administered because there's no staff available to do so (and I can't keep it myself because it's 'Hospital Policy'. - although last time I asked for a plaster there wasn't even a medical

---

6   From one of Col's diaries.

box!) Where the shower (a hose attached to the wall)
always runs cold/luke-warm-at-best.

It was a shame my home leave ended as it did. But
is it really a surprise I didn't want to come back?! To come
back to this; a locked ward, angry distressed patients,
restrictions that stifle and subdue me, not enough
exercise to legitimate proper eating, depression; I could go
on and on...

The much-longed-for move to Pathway House, when it came, was
not a success. We can categorically say that the seven months you
spent at Milton Park were the most unhappy in your life. Caring
for someone with your acute mental health conditions was never
going to be easy. Milton Park had your Complex Case Review
from Sussex, which clearly outlined all your needs. However, in
our view, they failed to address any of the fundamental issues in
it. I reproduce extracts and a summary from this:

**Complex Case Review, with a view to possible
referral to Specialist Placement panel**
Attendees: Colette, Parents of CM, Dr Pannu (Consultant Psychiatrist), Liz Hennessy (Senior SW, CC), Rebecca Simpson (SNP,
Autism, CCP)

- Colette has a diagnosis of High Functioning Autism and emotionally unstable personality disorder. Her ASD diagnosis is
  recent and has many treatments over the years focussed on
  her eating disorder, OCD, Alcohol Abuse and Anxiety.

- Despite previous multi-agency working under safeguarding
  (including police presence) and with the maximum possible

level of support and monitoring Colette has continued to be at risk of harm from others (including death) and risk of harm to herself by engaging in cycles of obsessive relationships with violently abusive and exploitative men. The obsessive nature of these attachments is significant and is part of her restricted intense interests... She also has severely impaired ability to evaluate and read other people. In spite of at least daily reminders of her vulnerability and reiterating to her the risks to self, Colette is unable to retain this information and protect herself.

- **Due to her Autism and impaired executive functioning she is unable to fully assess situations that could put her at risk of harm to herself.** She finds social engagement, friendships and relationships very difficult and does not have any friends...

- Colette has many skills and is a very talented writer and artist, her work is outstanding. She is (often) not able to engage in creating any pieces of work as she is tormented by having to rearrange her seating/desk area as she is obsessed with the proximity that items/structures have to each other.

Summary of current need

Colette requires an Autistic Spectrum Disorder placement that provides a level of protection but also has an inbuilt rehabilitative programme.

A capacity assessment may be required and deprivation of liberty safeguards will need to be considered.

Colette has tentatively agreed to consider a placement but has very impaired future imagination and therefore will need help and support to give meaningful consent to admission.

Your Complex Case Review runs to a full eight A4 pages. Any health care worker reading it should have been able to form an accurate view of you and your condition at that time. Staff at Milton Park (Lakeside) supposedly specialise in treating autism of all types. So how come you were to die, in such appalling and avoidable circumstances, after less than seven months in their 'experienced clinical therapeutic' care? Going through this is deeply upsetting for us. In hindsight we now realise that your placement at Milton Park was a huge and tragic mistake. But because it is so hard to find treatment for people with autism, once it is offered by so-called experts, of course parents trust them. That trust is often misplaced, as it was in our case. Painful though it is, it is vital to investigate what went wrong, so as to prevent the same failings happening again. Current tragedies, being exposed by the charity Inquest and the media, indicate that these failings are widespread and occur all the time.

There was no one simple cause in your case. No one person was standing there, holding a smoking gun that led directly to your death. The driver of the lorry that struck you was in no way at fault. It was, in our opinion, a toxic cocktail of accidents and negligence, along with lethal indifference, that killed you. A number of agencies were responsible.

One unforeseen factor was that Liz Hennessy, your care co-ordinator in Sussex, suffered a family bereavement in January, shortly after your admission. She took much-needed compassionate leave. She was off work until June. She knew you better than anyone and was our link to the staff at Milton Park. Her role was to keep in touch with and visit you, so as to make sure the placement was working. She was in effect monitoring your treatment. A replacement co-ordinator was appointed in early February but she did not meet you until May.

There should have been a Care Programme Approach (CPA) meeting within weeks of your admission. The care plan for your stay should have been discussed and decided on at that meeting. In Liz's absence this CPA did not take place until 19th May, four whole months later! By then the placement had totally broken down. The CPA, when it finally happened, didn't really discuss your treatment at all. In the event it was about giving you notice to quit and charging Sussex with finding an alternative placement for you.

But to our minds, the primary failings in your care were the responsibility of the clinic/care home and the local Approved Mental Health Professional service in Bedford, which was supposed to intervene when necessary. They were contacted on a number of occasions and failed to respond. You were in Milton Park's care and they let you take life-threatening risks. They were risks they'd been warned about, in your Complex Case Review. The chapters on the coroner's court will cover these failings in detail. However, at this stage it is necessary to review a summary of the issues that, in our opinion, made a full inquest into your death imperative.

- Your care co-ordinator's bereavement in January was tragic. A new co-ordinator was appointed in early February. But she did not meet you until the CPA in May. Why?

- The CPA itself was postponed several times by Sussex. The reason given each time was that a senior manager was never available. She didn't even attend when the CPA finally took place in May. Why did Sussex leave a patient unmonitored for so long?

- Milton Park is a hundred miles from Brighton. Why couldn't Sussex find a clinic closer by?

- Why did staff at Milton Park ignore the Complex Case Review's advice that you lacked capacity? Why did they leave you at such acute risk?

- Why did Milton Park organise so few activities for you that you ended up roaming the local area with no sense of purpose?

- Why did Milton Park allow you to stay out in local hotels at weekends, and on one occasion for *four consecutive nights*?

- Why did Milton Park let you leave the premises, at 8.30 am, without seeing anyone, after jumping from a bridge into the river, the previous day, with suicidal intent?

- The local AMHP service was contacted four times to come out and assess you. Why did they turn down all those requests? Two of them after the suicide attempt?

- Why in July did Milton Park threaten to evict you from Pathway House, onto the streets within 48 hours?

- Why did staff allow you to be missing from the campus, for 17 hours, on the day which led to your death?

- Why didn't Milton Park phone the police, with your special emergency code, as they were supposed to when you went missing?

The list goes on and on. It seemed logical to us that these questions must be answered if future avoidable deaths, like yours, are to be prevented. Failings must be openly addressed if they are to be put right. However, it turned out that what seemed logical to bereaved parents did not to various elements of the state...

Part IV

CHAPTER 23

Celebration and Confrontation

2016 was a year of turmoil. The world shook on its axis; certainties were trashed and burned, good people died for bad reasons. You had little interest in world affairs but the daily bombing and massacres of thousands of innocent women, men and children, in Aleppo, Syria, did get through to you. Brexit didn't interest you. You thought Trump was a total buffoon but you didn't live to see him in the White House. It wouldn't have surprised you though. You had zero respect for politics. It was people that mattered to you. You were appalled by Jo Cox's murder. It chimed with your view of women being crushed by male brutality. You identified with characters like Blanche DuBois, in *A Streetcar Named Desire*, being destroyed by Stanley. Victoria Wood, Caroline Aherne and the singer Prince, while not victims, were huge losses for you as well. But the greatest loss was the death of your beloved David Bowie. After The Rolling Stones, you admired him and his music more than that of any other. For your mother and me, 2016 was defined by one thing alone – your senseless death. As any bereaved parent would confirm, it was the single most shattering event of our lives. How could we grapple towards making any sense of that?

The entrance to West Norwood Cemetery is under a Gothic arch. It was consecrated in 1837. It was one of the first private landscaped burial grounds in London. It is now owned by the Borough of Lambeth. On the morning of Friday 19th August 2016 your hearse purred slowly under the arch and up the hill to the crematorium, housed in the old Dissenters' chapel. The small cortège followed. We felt that you, as a lifelong dissenter, would approve. Deciding on where your funeral should take place had been just one of the bureaucratic tasks to be carried out. Like getting an interim death certificate, appointing a funeral director. Closing down your bank account, standing orders, direct debits and benefit payments. The dull painful processes of erasing the official traces of your existence. We're not religious. Nor were you, in any conventional sense anyway, despite the fact that you'd always loved the Bible stories. A humanist service, of some kind, seemed the most honest proposition. There are lay celebrants who conduct humanist services. But we realised it would be next to impossible to explain to someone who'd never met you the idiosyncrasies of your character. In the end we decided to conduct the service ourselves in an attempt to convey the essence of you.

Colette was unique and increasingly at odds with what the world expected of her and frequently, utterly beyond its understanding. This must have been very painful and bewildering for her, albeit she had the love and care and protection of her family. But there was something superb about Colette, something dauntless as, in spite of all, she resolutely made her own path, directed by her own, what was to us, inaccessible logic.

Colette's short life might seem tragic to some but she lived it with such energy, almost with ferocity, and with such bursts of creativity and destructiveness that one can only admire the spirit with which she persisted, despite her seemingly unsolvable problems which, for Colette, were not so much problems as simply life. She was outside us all and there is a certain magnificence in that.[1]

Our close friend, the author Ursula Jones, wrote those words. She comes as close to capturing who you were, as anyone could. Sadly, due to a sudden illness she was unable to be there on the day. However, her tribute was read out to the assembled friends who packed the small chapel. Gill Todd and Norma from the Bethlem Eating Disorders Unit had come, as had Liz Hennessy, Mary and Kate from Sussex. And most touchingly of all, two of your fellow patients at the Bethlem, Gemma King and Caroline (Caz) Spray, were there. They had travelled miles to be there for you. Your sister Chloe, her partner Teddy, their two young sons and toddler daughter were there. As were aunts and cousins, your uncle Patrick who had always been supportive of you, and your cousin Nick, who had been like an older brother to you and your sister and who shared your interest in art. Many of the rest of the mourners were our friends who'd known you over the years. Amanda and I conducted the service and friends read pieces of your work. Chloe read excerpts from *Winnie-the-Pooh*, which you loved. But her own inner feelings are better expressed in a poem she wrote a few days after your death. Chloe is a journalist, she was deeply affected by her sister's death:

> Before I was the one with no time
> And you had too much.
> Too much time to think dark thoughts
> While I could barely think at all,
> Piled high with kids' washing and endless tea times
> Lovely, grubby, exhausting chaos.

---

1   Ursula Jones, writer, actress and close family friend.

I had to block you out
Your pain was deep, bottomless.
Now that's over, your time's run out
And there's nothing left to do
Except remember.
Kids' cries still stir me
But in between I have moments, glimpses of you,
So powerful I can't breathe.
I hear your voice, see your face and then you're gone.
And I cry.
C x²

The music was from some of your sixties favourites: Fleetwood Mac's 'Beautiful Child', Bob Dylan's 'She Belongs to Me' (a song about a girl who was an artist), and finishing with The Rolling Stones' '(I Can't Get No) Satisfaction'. The rock music filled the old chapel as we said goodbye to you in your raffia coffin and filed out on a wave of emotion.

The Prince Regent is a fine old Victorian pub in Herne Hill, near Brockwell Park. The sympathetic Liverpudlian landlord let us hire two of his large upstairs rooms and allowed us to have access the day before. We hung your paintings and your line drawings on the walls of one room, along with photos of you at various stages of your life. The pub served excellent food and wine in the other room. People wandered through and looked at your work and your photos in appreciative surprise. Most had no idea what a talented artist you were. We also placed printouts of your poems on tables. Our friends and relatives were engrossed in reading them. The atmosphere was warm and full of empathy. You'd never had an eighteenth or a twenty-first birthday party. You'd never had a

---

2   'Colette' poem by Chloe McCulloch, 2016.

graduation party, after university. This was your party, a celebration of your life. The room buzzed with conversations about you
and your extraordinary abilities. You would have been so chuffed.

*   *   *

Friends were considerate and supportive, but as we moved
into September, the reality of Colette's death was sinking in.
Questions of how this had been allowed to happen hung like
rotten fruit left unpicked on its tree. Still numbed by shock we
wondered where the answers would come from. Our daughter
had died whilst in the care of a private mental health care unit
commissioned by the NHS. Who was going to investigate? The
Cambridgeshire coroner, who had produced the interim death
certificate (she died just inside Cambridgeshire), told us that
the inquest would be Bedfordshire's responsibility. We were
informed that the Bedfordshire and Luton Coroner Service would
take over the case. We contacted the coroner's officer, who told us
that a date would be set shortly for the inquest. First the police
had to compile a collision report for the coroner. We discussed
the process with our friend Gerard, a retired lawyer, who had
worked in this area of the law. He reassured us that coroners'
understanding when dealing with bereaved families had much
improved in the last ten years. He didn't think we would need
legal representation. He suggested that I put together a detailed
chronology of events that took place while Colette was resident
at Milton Park. This was easily done as we had Amanda's detailed
handwritten diary. I completed the chronology on my laptop and
emailed it to the coroner. The coroner's officer acknowledged
receipt of the document, saying it would be helpful to have it.

Bedfordshire Police came and interviewed us about the accident. They had tested the driver's blood for alcohol and drugs

at the time. He was completely clear. They had examined his tachometer – he had not been speeding, nor had he exceeded his hours of driving. He was not at fault. Having heard this, we asked the police to let the driver know we were not holding him responsible in any way. The police showed us photos of the road, the articulated lorry and diagrams of paths of Colette and the vehicle. It was a cold, chilling experience but they were professional and appeared to know their stuff. They said they would produce their report and let us see it before the inquest, which was to take place on 8th December.

Meanwhile, two separate Serious Incident Reviews into Col's death were taking place. Sussex Partnership Trust and Milton Park both said they would carry out their own inquiries. This seemed to us like getting a criminal to investigate his own crimes rather than having the police investigate them. In the event the product of their reviews showed that we were right to have misgivings. Both internal reports were a travesty of the truth. Mistakes and failings were glossed over. What's more, they were both delivered months late. A separate safeguarding review was set up by the East London NHS Trust that ran Bedford's mental health services. This was a more in-depth process. Failings in Bedford's Approved Mental Health Professional service's actions came to light. At one meeting, when a member of the AMHP management was challenged about the failings, she said that were the situation to arise again her team would do exactly the same. There was a stunned silence in the room. Amanda and I were appalled. At the end of the meeting we were told that the investigation would now be escalated up to being a full Safeguarding Adults Review. I quote from the Care Act (2014) below:

Safeguarding Adult Boards (SABs) must arrange a Safeguarding Adult Review (SAR) when an adult in its area dies as a result of abuse or neglect, whether known or suspected, and there is concern that partner agencies could have worked together more effectively to protect the adult. This is a statutory responsibility. The overall purpose of a Safeguarding Adult Review is to promote learning and improve practice, not to re-investigate or to apportion blame.

While this was a welcome development in our search for the truth, the final sentence is the most important. It would not re-investigate what had gone wrong. It would have no power to ensure practices were changed; it could only recommend. We needed to establish what had gone wrong, in a court of law. The only way to do that is through a full inquest conducted by a coroner.

As its date of 8th December approached, Colette's inquest was postponed. The police had been unable to complete their collision report in time. The inquest was changed to become a Pre-Inquest Review (PIR – the acronyms go on and on I'm afraid!). Our retired lawyer friend Gerard told us this was quite good, as we would be able to calmly discuss the content of the postponed inquest and establish a relationship with the coroner. Gerard, who happened to live near the coroner's court, said he would come to the hearing with us and explain anything we didn't understand. None of us had met Coroner Ian Pears at this stage. We were all in for a surprise.

The Court House, Woburn Street, Ampthill, is a modern building set back from a tree-lined road leading out of the small town. The coroner's court is in a large light room with adjustable seating. At the moment the seats are arranged in rows, in two formal blocks, either side of a central aisle. The two blocks face a raised platform with a large chair. The chair is empty, waiting for the arrival of Coroner Pears. He is late. Amanda, Gerard and I sit in the right-hand block of seats, the rest of which are vacant.

Gerry Graham and one other from Milton Park sit alone in the left-hand block. A solitary lawyer, representing the lorry driver, sits a few rows behind them. Silence reigns. A clerk of the court then appears and says, 'All rise.' All six of us do.

Assistant Coroner Ian Pears sweeps in. He is in his fifties, with a brusque manner. He sits, and with a brief look down to us declares in a loud voice, 'I won't have any shouting in this court!'

He gives the court a supercilious scan. There are three of us in our seventies on one side and three middle-aged people on the other. Who did he imagine was going to start a riot?

He focuses his eyes on Amanda and me and, having confirmed who we are, bluntly states, 'Only one of you can speak, so decide which one. And you can only speak for three minutes!'

He goes on to pronounce, 'I want to make it clear from the start that I intend to treat this as a simple road traffic accident. Was the driver at fault or was it Colette? I am not concerned with why this accident happened, only how it happened. That is all that will concern my inquest. Mr McCulloch?'

He looks to me with sceptical eyes, inviting me to respond. I was astonished at his aggression. Family friendly? Gerard and I look to each other in disbelief. Through confusion and anger I speak, 'Well sir, if you are only concerned with the how, perhaps you should investigate HOW Colette came to be on the A1 at 2.30 in the morning when she should have been in her clinic/care home being looked after? Perhaps you should investigate HOW trained mental health staff allowed this to happen?'

Pears is dismissive: 'What you're saying is not a how but a why. If you want those questions answered I suggest you go to the Care Quality Commission. They are not matters that concern this court.'

He knows very well that the Care Quality Commission (CQC) has little jurisdiction compared with a coroner's court. He goes on to say that he envisages a short inquest of a few hours, early next year. He then dismisses the court. The entire hearing has taken twenty minutes.

We are outside the court building reeling in shock. It feels as though we've been thumped in the solar plexus. Gerard takes us to his car and says that he has never witnessed a coroner behaving like that. He drives us to Flitwick Station nearby. He tells us that we will have to find proper legal representation, at once, if we are to achieve justice for our daughter. He knows the right firm. He will contact them on our behalf.

We sit on the train in shocked disbelief at what has just happened. Our faith in British justice is in tatters. That man simply wanted to sweep Colette's death under a legal carpet as quickly as he could. We found out later that Pears was getting through as many as six inquests in a day. Six people's lives being given no more than an hour of his time! In our case it was only four months since Colette's death. But there wasn't a hint of concern for us, or our loss. He was aggressive towards us from the very beginning. Interestingly, when our newly instructed solicitor came to ask for a recording of the hearing (which is our right to have), she received an extraordinary reply. She was told that the first three or four minutes were missing – the minutes when Pears was at his most aggressive. When she asked why they were missing, she was told there had been a fault on the recording machine, which had righted itself later on. It had apparently never happened before!

We get home and are still in shock. We fall into bed exhausted. Amanda becomes quite ill. She cannot stop being sick. In the morning I have to go to our GP to get a pill to stop her retching. How could a coroner treat bereaved parents in such an inhumane manner? And more importantly what hope could we have of getting any justice from him?

CHAPTER 24

The Wheels of Justice

We were beginning to understand the immense powers that coroners wield in their own courts. They appear to be answerable to no one. It was mid-December; 2016 was coming to an end. It had been an awful year for our family. Colette's time in care at Milton Park had been an almost constant series of crises. She'd frequently been at risk. She spent days going AWOL from the clinic/care home, culminating in whole weekends staying out in cheap hotels, drinking. She had made one serious suicide attempt by jumping from a bridge into the river. All attempts to have her assessed under the Mental Health Act were screened out by the Bedford Approved Mental Health Professional (AMHP) service. Without ever meeting her, or reading her notes, they decided her issue were purely with alcohol; this despite her diagnosis of autism.

Then in July, she was killed at 3 am in the morning, walking on the A1. She had been missing, without permission, from the clinic/care home for well over twelve hours before they did anything to find her. They did not even alert the police despite having an agreed emergency procedure to do so. Milton Park had been taking huge fees for her care for seven months. Since her death we hadn't received a single communication from them offering even an acknowledgement of what had happened. No phone call, no email, not even a bland 'sorry for your loss' letter. They chose to ignore us totally now she was dead. (When they did eventually call us, six months later, it was only because Gerry Graham, the manager, wished to inform us that we could not have Col's medical records. Later, our solicitors told us it was our legal right to have them.) We now realised that a full inquest into Colette's death was essential if we were to prevent this happening to someone else. However, Assistant Coroner Pears seemed determined to treat her avoidable death as a simple road traffic accident. What could be done? It is extremely difficult to challenge a ruling made by a coroner. There's no straightforward appeals procedure. The omens weren't good.

Then we met Merry Varney. Our friend Gerard had written to her on our behalf. She asked us to see her at the Leigh Day offices in Clerkenwell on the morning of 21st December. Merry is a bundle of energy and commitment. She radiates optimism but with a sharp probing mind. She's an astute human rights lawyer. This meeting was to change our lives. I can do no better than to endorse a statement from one of her many satisfied clients.

> Just when we thought there was no hope we found Merry. She was the light at the end of our tunnel.[1]

Merry had done her homework on Coroner Pears. He had form. We weren't the first bereaved family he had upset and we wouldn't be the last. She listened carefully as we related Colette's story to her. She was in no doubt that Colette's human rights had been violated by the treatment (and lack of treatment) that

---

1   Leigh Day (2020) *Merry Varney* [client testimonial]. Accessed on 23/06/2020 at www.leighday.co.uk/Our-experts/partners-at-ld/Merry-Varney.

she received. Firstly, several agencies were accountable in her opinion. Col was in state care, so Sussex Partnership Trust was answerable. Secondly, the clinic/care home, which was directly responsible for her day-to-day treatment, must be accountable. Thirdly, the AMHP service, who were supposed to oversee that treatment, were clearly at fault. Since Col's right to life had been violated, in effect by the state, there should be a full inquest. Thus Article 2 of the European Convention on Human Rights would be engaged. That being the case we would qualify for some legal aid for the inquest, Merry told us. But first she foresaw a legal battle with Coroner Pears to achieve Article 2. We would require the services of a highly qualified barrister, practised in this area. That would be expensive. First Merry would write to Pears and ask him to widen the scope of the inquest.

Meanwhile, a further Serious Incident Review was carried out by East London NHS Trust, which runs Bedford's mental health services, looking into the failings in their AMHP service. The service had been asked four times to come and assess Colette's mental state. They refused on each occasion. Dr Cathie O'Driscoll, the psychiatrist writing this review, identified serious systemic failings in the service. She ruled out apportioning blame to any individual for the failings. Still, it was useful ammunition.

Doughty Street is a broad tree-lined road of Georgian terraced houses. Charles Dickens wrote *Oliver Twist* while he was living at number 48. A few doors down, number 54 houses the eponymous Doughty Street Chambers. Many well-known QCs are part of the chambers, including Geoffrey Robertson, Dame Helena Kennedy and Keir Starmer, before politics took him away. We were meeting our QC for the first time. Amanda and I approached the building with some trepidation. What were we walking into? Were we getting out of our depth? Should we just leave it to the various inquiries and see what happened? However, on meeting Caoilfhionn Gallagher QC, our doubts and fears were soon dismissed. Caoilfhionn is a force. Her open and enthusiastic manner belies a fierce intelligence. She got straight down to business. We would never get justice for Col unless we took on Coroner Pears. She looked to Merry who nodded in agreement. Caoilfhionn then proceeded to outline the entire case, and all its ramifications, with the velocity of a turbo-charged machine gun. The gist of it was that Pears must change the upcoming inquest to a second PIR. If he continued to limit scope, deny an Article 2 inquest and refuse to call our witnesses, he must recuse himself (i.e. step down). If he did not agree to this, we could take him to Judicial Review (JR). A JR is an immense undertaking. Amanda and I would in effect be taking a coroner to the High Court.

The risks are massive but it's the only way that you can challenge a coroner. The official Ministry of Justice (MOJ) figures for Judicial Reviews are hardly encouraging. They state that only 1% of cases are successful.[2] However, UK Human Rights Blog disputes this. They say that figure is based on the number of complaints lodged. However, if you consider those that are actually heard, it rises to 36%[3] which, while still challenging, is a lot better than 1%! It is interesting that the MOJ put out the dispiriting 1% figure. One can only imagine they don't want to encourage people to go to Judicial Review. The law does not like being questioned – something we were to find out in no uncertain terms.

Back at Doughty Street, Merry admitted that our costs alone for a JR would be £30,000, and that could double if we lost. Pears had already signalled to her that, if we lost, he might demand

---

2   UK Human Rights Blog (2015) *The True Statistics Behind Judicial Review's Success Rates*. Accessed on 23/06/2020 at https://ukhumanrightsblog. com/2015/03/23/the-true-statistics-behind-judicial-reviews-success-rates.

3   *Ibid*.

we pay his costs as well – not normal practice amongst coroners. With a statistical chance of only 36% that was scary. Plaintiffs have to pay the full costs of a Judicial Review themselves, no legal aid is available for such an action. So we were potentially facing a bill of £60,000 before the inquest had even started. But Caoilfhionn and Merry reassured us that it would not come to this. The two women were confident that once confronted, Coroner Pears would back down. We'd seen him in action and weren't so sure...

At this time, Merry had received no commitment from Pears to widen the scope. A few weeks later, having received the partial recording of the first PIR from the coroner's officer, Merry wrote to Pears again. All his rude bullying from the first few minutes of the hearing in December was missing from the official court recording. She wrote:

Dear Sir,

... Our clients have grave concerns about the manner in which they were treated at the previous PIR and having received the benefit of legal advice, have been further distressed to learn that the content of what they were told regarding the law on scope of Inquests was partially incorrect.

The Ministry of Justice's Guide to Coroner Services sets out a section 1.1 'general standards' that families can expect during a Coroner's Investigation and of particular relevance states that the Coroner's Office will:

'provide a welcoming and safe environment and treat you with fairness, respect and sensitivity'.

It is not our clients' view, nor the view of an independent attendee or us as legal representatives having listened to the recording that this standard has been upheld.

Further details are set out below and we are instructed to seek transfer of the Inquest to another Coroner given our clients have lost all confidence in their daughter's death being fully and fairly investigated.

It is hugely regrettable and of grave concern that the recording provided of the PIR does not cover the entire hearing. No meaningful explanation has been provided for this omission and the recording itself contains no explanation to note that the recording is partial.

Recording PIRs and Inquest hearings is a mandatory obligation pursuant to Rule 26 Coroners (Inquest) Rules 2013 and Guidance sheet no.4 requires a Coroner to 'take reasonable steps to ensure that the device is working at all times'.

Merry goes on to state that my argument in the court about the importance of how Colette came to be on the A1, at the time, was perfectly valid. Pears had ruled it out. Merry demolished much of what Pears had said on 8th December and objected to his delaying tactics. She concludes with:

Further, in many Inquests the concerns of the bereaved family are of negligent care, including failures to provide reasonable care, failures to act in accordance with policy and good practice etc, and it is of utmost concern that our clients were told such concerns could not be the subject matter of an Inquest.

Request to recuse
In light of the above concerns our clients respectfully request that you transfer this matter to a different Coroner for onward conduct.

Given the proximity of the PIR we would be grateful for a prompt reply.

Please note that we have copied this complaint to the Judicial Conduct Investigation Office and confirmed we shall be in touch further with them if the matter cannot be resolved to our clients' satisfaction following this complaint.

We look forward to hearing from you.

Yours faithfully

Leigh Day

We never received a full reply to this letter. On 14th March we are back in the Ampthill Coroner's Court. It is a second PIR as Caoilfhionn had requested. This time the place is bristling with solicitors and barristers. East London NHS Trust who ran the AMHP service is represented. Milton Park is represented. Their consultant psychiatrist is represented separately. Sussex Partnership Trust is represented, as is the lorry driver. Caoilfhionn and Merry are there for us. A schedule has not been produced (normal practice is that it should be) so we are uncertain how Pears would proceed. Would he accept our request that he stand aside and let another coroner hear the case?

We soon find out. Pears has no intention of engaging Article 2 for this inquest.

Pears' bullying manner has no effect on Caoilfhionn; she is unfazed. She sets out our stall with clinical precision. Colette died an avoidable death, while in state care, and that constituted a fundamental breach of her human rights. Thus it is clear that this should be a human rights, Article 2 inquest. All the legal representatives of the other interested parties accept Caoilfhionn's argument. But Pears hotly disputes it. During one angry exchange he accuses Caoilfhionn of trying to blackmail him. There is a stunned silence in the court. She fixes him with eyes of steel. She lowers her voice and speaks with serious deliberation:

'I think sir you might like to reconsider that remark. You have just accused a Queen's Counsel, in open court, of committing blackmail. I suggest you take that back.'

After an uneasy pause, Pears grudgingly does so. He then takes a short recess of fifteen minutes to consider our request for him to recuse himself. He returns to say that he will not do so. He will be in touch shortly with a schedule for the inquest. He asks all interested parties present to put in their submissions. He then makes an extraordinary request that all the lawyers should send their submissions to each other rather than to him. He is clogged up with letters as it is. He is not 'a post box' he declares. There is another awkward silence. The clerk of the court is forced to intervene. She points out that all communication has to be via the coroner, by law. Again, Pears grudgingly accepts this.

However, our chances of achieving a fair inquest seem more remote than ever. It is now clear that Pears will not stand aside and will never grant us the open inquest we require. It is also clear that he has adopted an adversarial position against us, our case and our legal representatives. It looks as though the only path left will be a Judicial Review against him.

Amanda and I arrive back home that evening. We are very conflicted about going to Judicial Review. Would we be able to cope with the stress – emotional, physical and financial? A coroner is supposed to be impartial. The last thing we wanted was to go to war with him. But it seemed there was no choice.

CHAPTER 25

Letters Before Action

Sometimes
When you cannot trust yourself,
When inhabiting your own skin
Is mortally repellent
You need to put your trust
In Something else.
Religion does the trick
For some.
A person met or
Conceived in the mind
Might steady your reality.[1]

'Be To Be' was one of her more optimistic poems; this is just an excerpt. We needed all the optimism we could find and meeting Merry and Caoilfhionn certainly did steady our resolve. However, a path forward in our search for justice still seemed out of reach. Merry put in the submissions for a full inquest to Coroner Pears. We waited for a response. March passed and we waited. By mid-April we had still heard nothing. On Merry's advice we

---

1   First verse of 'Be To Be' by Colette.

wrote to the JCIO (Judicial Conduct Investigations Office) to escalate our official complaint about Pears' behaviour and his alleged bias against us:

Dear Sirs,

Escalation of Complaint regarding HM Coroner Ian Pears
We are writing to you subsequent to our complaint made directly to HM Coroner Ian Pears on 7th March this year, copied to you. Since then we have had a further PIR on 14th March, in which Mr. Pears, without any prior notice, addressed our complaint in open court... A number of specific points remain unanswered:

- He has in no way acknowledged that his manner in the first PIR did not accord to section 1.1 of the 'general standards' in the Guide to Coroner Services. He apologised only to say 'If am perceived to be rude... I am what I am...it was not intentional'. We do not find this reassuring and therefore wish our complaint to be escalated.

- He gave no explanation for the missing first minutes of the court recording other than to say 'the system wasn't working for some unknown reason'. This is very unsatisfactory given that Mr. Pears was, to our mind, particularly abrasive in those opening minutes.

- He has given no explanation for his failure to 'provide a welcoming and safe environment...and act with compassion'. It was our first experience of a coroner's court and we felt we were in a hostile environment, not a welcoming one.

- He does not acknowledge that he set a narrow 'scope' for the Inquest. He stated in the first PIR, 'All I will be looking at is the day of the death... I will be looking at this simply from the road traffic accident point of view'. In the second PIR he claimed that he left it 'open'. But this is clearly not the case. We have listened to the recording several times and we find the Coroner's denial very concerning.

- We understand that the Judicial Conduct and Investigations Office cannot consider legal issues but we do ask that the dismissive way in which we were treated, as bereaved family members with no legal knowledge, be considered.

- He produced no agenda for the legal teams in the second PIR. He had not circulated submissions to them either. Again this seems inadequate.

... Our sole reason for pursuing this Inquest, is to have the events that led to Colette's death, openly and fairly investigated. The unnecessary death of a beloved daughter is hard enough to bear but to have it investigated by someone whose manner is so dismissive and lacking in empathy, makes it almost impossible. It is our fervent wish that a tragedy like this will not happen to another vulnerable mental health patient. Given the history of this case, it is our belief that Mr. Pears is ill equipped to carry out this duty.

It is for all of the above reasons that we ask the JCIO to investigate our complaint and we feel another Coroner should take over Colette's inquest.

Yours sincerely

Andrew and Amanda McCulloch

The hope was that the JCIO would uphold our complaint thus avoiding a Judicial Review. We should have known better; as we said earlier, the law does not like having its own criticised. In June the JCIO turned down our complaint. Apparently there was not sufficient evidence of bias against us to have the coroner removed. That left us with the sole option of appealing to the Legal Ombudsman against the JCIO decision.

Meanwhile, through April and May, Suzaan Jenkinson and Tony Alston (of ELFT) were continuing with an S42 enquiry[2] into failings in Colette's care. In particular they were investigating how she was threatened with immediate eviction from Milton Park only days before she died. In mid-July 2016, Fiona Joyner (head of Pathway House) sent a new support worker, at 9 in the morning, to tell Col that she was to be excluded from the premises within 48 hours. She was to be left in the care of the police. Colette rang us. She was hysterical. She did what she always did when she was overwhelmed by her emotions – she ran away. As Fiona Joyner should have known she would. She went missing until late that night. This eviction was only stopped because we reported the threat to the Care Quality Commission. They told us that such an exclusion from a care home would be illegal. Fiona Joyner backed down. Now, almost a year later, we attended a meeting with Suzaan Jenkinson, Tony Alston, Fiona Joyner and others. The police were represented. The officer stated that they knew absolutely nothing about Ms Joyner's plan and under no circumstances would they have agreed to it.

'Why would we take responsibility for a mental health patient, when she was already in a care home?'

Sadly this S42 enquiry was halted later and rolled into the main SAR. Which meant the threatened eviction and its implications were never satisfactorily investigated.

Nothing then happened over the summer. Pears was not responding to letters from Merry. He continued to delay any decision about widening scope or engaging Article 2. He complained

---

2   An S42 is any action that is taken (or instigated) by a local authority, under Section 42 of the Care Act 2014.

that we were late with our submissions. Merry demolished that argument with a comprehensive list of submissions sent by Leigh Day to him – all within the agreed time frame. He didn't comment. But he did extend the deadline for Bedford AMHP to lodge their submissions, thus delaying the process further. Then at the end of October, *over seven months after the PIR*, Pears finally announced he would agree to an Article 2 inquest. However, he would not widen the scope of the inquest to include witnesses vital to our case. This was not acceptable.

By now Pears had employed a legal firm, LGSS Law, to represent him at the looming Judicial Review. As we have said, his costs were covered by the state. We had to pay our own. What's more, Pears was now determined to carry out his threat and make us pay his costs as well, if we lost. Merry and Caoilfhionn put together a detailed, ten-page letter to LGSS Law, outlining our grounds for complaint against Pears and his actions. It was sent on 7th November 2017. This is the short summary at the end of the letter. We are the proposed claimants, Pears is the proposed defendant:

Action sought

As indicated above, the proposed Claimants seek:

a. Immediate confirmation of the proposed Defendant's position regarding costs in any judicial review; and

b. Agreement of the proposed Defendant to recuse himself from this Inquest.

In the event that you agree to recuse yourself, please confirm you shall, within 7 days, issue a direction to a Senior Coroner in another area in accordance with s.2 Coroners and Justice Act 2009.

Please be aware we shall also be writing with copies of this and other relevant correspondence to the Chief Coroner to ask for exercise of his powers under s.3 Coroners and Justice Act 2009...

Further, should the proposed Defendant not agree to recuse himself, the proposed Claimants seek confirmation that the scope of the Inquest will be extended in accordance with the above and that the factual matrix is withdrawn. Failing this, a judicial review will be issued without further notice.

Reply time

We consider a response within 7 days is reasonable in all the circumstances and we look forward to hearing from you within this timeframe.

Yours faithfully

Leigh Day

By also sending the letter to the Chief Coroner we hoped to increase pressure on Pears. We had to bring this matter to a head. Either Pears stepped aside or we must take him to the High Court. On Leigh Day's advice, that it was necessary, we started a crowdfunding campaign to help us pay for the Judicial Review.

In early November, we attended a book launch for *Justice for Laughing Boy*, Dr Sara Ryan's moving and revelatory account of how her son Connor died while in care and her subsequent battle for justice. It was an inspiring event. Caoilfhionn Gallagher spoke along with Sara and others. We met a number of journalists there, including Michael Buchanan from the BBC. We linked up with George Julian who'd masterminded the #JusticeforLaughingBoy Twitter campaign. She offered to come on-board and help us. We had already talked to Amelia Hill at *The Guardian*. She followed up and wrote an excellent in-depth article about Colette's case, the failings in her care and our dispute with the coroner. It appeared in *The Guardian* on 12th November 2017 and can still be accessed online. This short excerpt deals with the nub of our argument:

> After almost a year of pressure from the family's lawyers at Leigh Day solicitors and their barristers at Doughty Street Chambers, Pears agreed to marginally widen the inquiry. He is still, however, refusing to call witnesses that her parents say are vital to discovering the truth, including themselves and Colette's care co-ordinator from Sussex NHS.[3]

Now this was in the public domain it was in effect a declaration of war. We had also lodged an appeal to the Legal Ombudsman against the JCIO decision. We felt that our complaint to the JCIO about Pears should not have been dismissed. The pressure was mounting but, as Christmas approached, once again everything went quiet. Once again we waited...

*   *   *

2018. A new year, but no new coroner. The JCIO did not support our case against Pears. The Legal Ombudsman turned down our complaints. It seemed that Coroner Pears accusing our QC of committing blackmail in court was merely 'an unfortunate outburst'. The Legal Ombudsman made no comment about the recording of the hearing being incomplete. Pears then, for no good reason, decided to further delay by cancelling the date of the scheduled PIR from May to late June.

---

3   Hill, A. (2017) 'Family of autistic woman killed in traffic accident demand coroner's replacement.' *The Guardian*, 12 November. Accessed on 07/05/2020 at www.theguardian.com/uk-news/2017/nov/12/family-of-autistic-woman-killed-in-traffic-accident-demand-coroners-replacement-colette-mcculloch.

Early April we had a meeting at Doughty Street. Caoilfhionn, junior barrister Sam Jacobs, Merry Varney, Amanda and I attended. Pears' June date for the PIR was not possible for us. I was scheduled to have a knee operation then. The date was also not possible for other interested parties. This meant that there was no chance of holding it before the summer holiday break. We had now run out of patience. After *eighteen months* of hundreds of emails, long delays and acrimonious wrangling with Pears, we had got nowhere. We all agreed, at the Doughty Street meeting, that we must finally go ahead with the Judicial Review.

Merry wrote a conclusive 'Letter Before Action' listing all the incompetence, all the delays and obstructions that we claimed Pears was responsible for. It was a damning indictment of the way Pears had conducted Col's inquest, to date. It was duly sent to his lawyers. On 9th May we held a press conference at Doughty Street Chambers announcing our action. George Julian live-tweeted the whole event. (The speed of her tweeting is something to behold.) She went on to start #JusticeforCol on Twitter for us. It was an effective way of getting the story out into the public domain. At the same time we redoubled our crowdfunding through the organisation CrowdJustice. Hundreds of supporters came on-board. We raised over £15,000 towards the cost of the review. But more importantly, by having so many supporters, we built up a powerful campaign attracting interest from press, TV and radio. Our fight to get a new coroner to investigate Colette's death without fear or favour became, briefly, national news. We have, in large part, our CrowdJustice supporters to thank for that achievement. Some were friends of many years who had known Colette. Others were people who had suffered similar tragedies. Many more were just sympathetic people who read about Colette's case and generously became involved. We gave interviews to the BBC, ITV, and local and national radio programmes. There were articles in *The Times* and a number of other papers. Damien Gayle in *The Guardian* on 10th May 2018 hit the spot with an article headlined:

**Family seek to replace 'sarcastic' coroner
after autistic daughter died**
Lawyers for Amanda and Andy McCulloch, whose daughter Colette was hit by a lorry after she walked out of Pathway House, Bedford in the early hours of 28 July 2016, have accused Ian Pears, the acting senior coroner for Bedfordshire and Luton, of unacceptable delays and bias against the family.

Merry Varney, a partner in the human rights department at Leigh Day, who is representing the family, said: 'Inquests are often the main, if not only, route a bereaved family have to truth and accountability in a public arena and where there is a formal mechanism to prevent future deaths...the McCullochs are asking the court to ensure Colette, a vulnerable adult who died in care, receives the inquest she deserves.'[4]

Two weeks later, on 24th May, Merry Varney at Leigh Day received a letter from Pears' legal representatives. The gist of it was that Pears, to avoid any suggestion of bias against us, would recuse himself. A replacement coroner would be appointed. Victory! This meant that now, nearly two years after Colette's death, we could start the inquest process into what went wrong in her treatment. In Winston Churchill's words: 'It is not even the beginning of the end. But it is, perhaps, the end of the beginning.'

---

4 Gayle, D. (2018) 'Family seek to replace "sarcastic" coroner after autistic daughter died.' *The Guardian*, 10 May. Accessed on 07/05/2020 at www.theguardian.com/society/2018/may/10/family-seek-to-replace-sarcastic-coroner-after-autistic-daughter-died.

CHAPTER 26

Action

Early autumn. It's less than four months since Pears departed. He'd done so following the escalation of our complaints that he showed bias against your human rights. We had been saying that for months. Our complaints had been turned down by the Judicial Conduct Investigations Office, and the Legal Ombudsman. In the end it was only by threatening Pears with legal action that we made him stand aside.

Now on 13th September 2018 we meet the replacement Coroner Martin Oldham. He is holding his first PIR to decide the details of your inquest. We are back at the beginning – except with a new coroner. In June, as soon as he was appointed, Merry had written to Martin Oldham with our submissions. The legal representatives for Milton Park and the other interested parties did the same. Mr Oldham quickly got to grips with the last two years of email traffic and paperwork.

We enter the Ampthill courtroom once more. Everything looks different. The seating layout has been changed since our last visit. The coroner's chair is no longer raised on a plinth looking down on us all. Martin Oldham is seated on the same level as the rest of us. The interested parties, their legal representatives and the public sit in a large semicircle looking to the witness stand and the coroner. That gives the whole proceedings a more open and egalitarian feel. It's clear there is a new regime at work. Martin Oldham starts by apologising that it has taken so long to get this process underway. Official government advice states that an inquest should take place within six months of a death. It is now over two years since you died. After acknowledging the distress this delay must have caused, Martin Oldham confirms that it will of course be an Article 2, human rights inquest. He makes it clear that, in his experience, the person at the centre of an investigation like this is you, Colette, the victim. He asks that at the inquest, now scheduled for March 2019, one of us your parents should open the proceedings by telling the court about your character and who you were. He explains that his experience at the Hillsborough inquests has taught him that the victims must be seen as human beings with unique individual lives that mattered. Then at the end of the inquest he will ask one of us to sum up the proceedings, from our parental viewpoint.

He goes on to state that he recognises the need to widen the scope, exactly as we'd asked of Pears. He will call all the witnesses that our lawyers have asked for; many of whom his predecessor had refused to call. He goes further and says he will call two expert witnesses, specialists in the psychology and treatment of autism in women. He recognises that it is necessary to understand your condition in order to investigate your care and your needs. The inquest is set to be seven days, over three weeks. (Pears had originally suggested that it would barely last one morning, with probably just two or three witnesses.) The court only sits three days a week. The case will open on Wednesday 6th March and conclude on Thursday 21st March.

A cold March morning. Ampthill is an attractive little market town in Mid Bedfordshire. It is about forty miles north of London. Its railway station closed in 1959. The easiest way to get there is a train from St Pancras to Flitwick, then a cab the last few miles to the courthouse. We travel with our legal team. Merry, her assistant Dan, and Sam Jacobs, our barrister from Doughty Street Chambers, who had taken over from Caoilfhionn. We will have a family room at the court, where we can talk freely.

We all get out of the taxi and walk towards the now-familiar Ampthill Coroner's Court. We can hardly believe it – your inquest is finally happening. Two years and eight months after your death on that bleak unlit tarmac carriageway. This is an emotional moment for us. Amanda and I approach the glass doors with trepidation – this place has bad memories. However, George Julian and other friends are already there waiting. It is heartening to see friendly faces. The journey to Ampthill, from almost anywhere, is difficult. There is no café near the courthouse for refreshments. So we thank all your supporters who battled through and attended, armed with thermoses and sandwiches. Several, including your sister Chloe, made the journey on more than one occasion.

We've decided between us that Amanda is to address the court first, explaining your life and struggles with mental health. Struggles, in large part, caused by your autistic spectrum condition. George Julian is all set to live-tweet the whole inquest from this first day. She has done this at previous inquests – the first one being Connor Sparrowhawk's back in 2015. It is now an accepted practice in most courts. She gives no views in her live-tweeting. It is straightforward reportage and an excellent way of updating your followers. We had asked permission for her to do so in this inquest. There seemed to be no problem. But as soon as Coroner Oldham opens proceedings Paul Spencer, barrister for Milton Park/Lakeside/Brookdale Care/Tracscare/Accomplish (described on his chambers' website as 'a very reassuring

barrister and a cool customer; nothing takes him by surprise'),
lodges an objection. He claims Ms Julian has shown bias in previous cases she has live-tweeted. Sam Jacobs challenges this saying
that George only gives her opinions in her personal blogs. Her
live-tweeting will be on #JusticeforCol, a professional account.
It would be purely factual. George confirms to the coroner that
her private views will not be aired. Martin Oldham rules in her
favour and allows the tweeting. He points out that technology
moves on; ten years ago mobile phones weren't allowed in court.
Now everyone here has one. He is keen that the process be as
open and accessible as possible. Round one to you, Col.

Amanda then takes the stand. She gives a moving account
of your character; who you were, how you thought, the anxieties that plagued you. But above all your bravery, humour and
creativity. (I hope we have conveyed some of this in the body
of the book.) Coroner Oldham listens with interest. He had
already asked to read pieces of your poetry, see your paintings
and drawings. It is clear he has done so, been impressed by
them and wonders where this creativity came from. Amanda
explains how both your writing and your painting were your
way of releasing your innermost emotions. As you yourself say
in your autobiography:

> For brief periods, as I have sat in this hospital ward and
> typed, the words that I have brought together to form
> sentences that might translate my feelings, my thoughts
> swim before me like a billion little fish waiting to be caught.
> My spirit has fled the stubborn enclosures of my body
> and rested upon the page before you now. In this sense
> I have managed to escape the confines of my limiting
> illness. I have travelled fields of barley, roamed the streets

of Paris, kissed a prince in Venice. In my mind I have
penetrated the books I love.[1]

Your world of make believe, your stories were how you made
sense of the alien world around you. Your unique personality
came, quite rightly, to be a presence throughout the seven days
of the hearing. The remainder of the first day was taken up with
the police reports being read out. They described the events
surrounding your death that we've already related.

There are four main strands that need to be investigated at the
inquest. They involve Sussex Partnership Trust's responsibilities,
the AMHP service's responsibilities, and Milton Park's and their
psychiatrist Dr Oluwatayo's responsibilities. Then separately the
evidence from the two expert witnesses the coroner has called.
Representing the interested parties is a bank of highly qualified barristers and their legal teams, backed by almost limitless
funds, supplied by the state or private insurance schemes. It is all
of them versus us, bereaved parents fighting for justice. Let no
one claim an inquest is not adversarial. Those lawyers are being
paid to protect financial interests, not the interests of truth.
David and Goliath spring to mind.

But fortunately in this case 'David' has Sam Jacobs and Merry
Varney to go into battle for him. Sam's questioning is detailed
and persistent. He probes away digging out the truth. His grasp
of detail is impressive.

Sussex Partnership Trust witnesses are first to give evidence and be questioned. Liz Hennessy, your care co-ordinator,
gave a full account of your history with her. She came to your
funeral back in 2016. At the wake reception Liz told us that she
had learned more about autism from you than anyone. She had

---

1   From Colette's autobiography, written while in the Bethlem hospital.

co-authored your Complex Case Review, which established that you often lacked capacity. Liz's evidence to Coroner Oldham was clear in confirming that diagnosis. Capacity is one of the main issues to arise in the inquest. I will explore the Mental Capacity Act as and when it arises.

Claire Williams, Service Manager at Sussex, in effect Liz's boss, was next to be questioned by Sam Jacobs. She was asked about why nobody from Sussex had visited you in your first five months at Milton Park? Also why was there no continuity of care after Liz Hennessy had to take compassionate leave? She said that there was continuity. She claimed the replacement co-ordinator had a relationship with Colette and was well equipped to take over her care.

She admitted it was unfortunate it took so long for anyone to visit Milton Park and arrange a CPA. This sounded plausible until the replacement care co-ordinator, Stephanie Hunt, was later questioned by Coroner Oldham, via video link.

'Had you met Colette, Ms Hunt?'

'No sir, I met her for the first time in May 2016 at her CPA.'

In other words, she was your care co-ordinator for nearly four months. She didn't know you and had never met you. Hardly continuity of care! We understand that NHS mental health services are under enormous pressure but that just isn't good enough. It wasn't Ms Hunt's fault, it was due to systemic failings in the Trust's organisation. Given their inadequate internal review of their services, we maintain there is a huge need of improvement of Sussex Partnership Trust's mental health services.

*　　*　　*

The second main issue at the inquest was related to your capacity or lack of it. Milton Park's defence of letting you stay out in cheap hotels and leaving you to wander with no supervision is that you were capable of making your own decisions about what you did. Witness after witness from Pathway House, when questioned, just repeated the mantra 'she had Capacity'. It emerged under questioning that many of these witnesses had only a sketchy idea of what having capacity means. That is not surprising: they were support workers with no qualifications. Your key worker was a young woman around twenty years old who only had a qualification in 'Health & Safety'. You used to help her write your own reports and your care plans. She did not understand your autism and it was not likely she would have any knowledge of complex mental health law.

Here is a short summary of the Mental Capacity Act (2005):

The **Mental Capacity Act 2005** provides a statutory framework to empower and protect vulnerable people who are not able to make their own decisions. It makes it clear who can take decisions, in which situations, and how they should go about this. It enables people to plan ahead for a time when they may lose **capacity**.

The Complex Case Review of 2015 had made it very clear that you lacked capacity at various times. I quote a short extract from this review, which our barrister Sam Jacobs used in your inquest:

- … She also has severely impaired ability to evaluate and read other people. In spite of at least daily reminders of her vulnerability and reiterating to her the risks to self, Colette is unable to retain this information and protect herself. She has often sought out these dangerous partners, driven by her intense and obsessive interest in having a 'relationship'.

- Due to her Autism and impaired executive functioning she is unable to fully assess situations that could put her at risk of harm to herself...

All staff from Milton Park insisted you had capacity, which justified their leaving you to wander and be at risk. Under questioning from Sam Jacobs, all witnesses from Milton Park – from Dr Oluwatayo, the responsible clinician, through to the most inexperienced support workers – parroted that 'yes Colette had capacity'. Was it a coincidence that Accomplish employed a public relations company called PLMR (Political Lobbying & Media Relations) to attend each day of the inquest? We had crossed swords with Nathan Hollow, PLMR's account executive, before when he tried to stop publication of one of Amelia Hill's *Guardian* articles. He threatened legal action. Amelia Hill told him to go ahead. He backed down. Now at the inquest he was keeping a close eye on proceedings. It seemed symptomatic that Milton Park/Accomplish was spending so much of their resources on a public relations firm rather than on care and treatment in their 'specialist clinic'. PLMR caters for high-profile politicians, etc. Their services don't come cheap. It is worth noting that the majority of patients at Milton Park are funded by the NHS. Thus public money is being used to buy the services of a private PR company. We will return later to Milton Park's role in your avoidable death.

*   *   *

The third major issue, under scrutiny at the inquest, was why you were never assessed under the Mental Health Act? Despite the fact that you frequently put yourself at severe risk, once attempting suicide, nobody questioned your mental equilibrium.

Six months of increasingly dangerous behaviour, while in a mental health institution, and nobody did anything. This series of failings involves witnesses from the Approved Mental Health Professional service and Milton Park. Things were going seriously wrong with your placement at Pathway House almost as soon as you moved there. You had already started staying out at a local hotel on a weekend. On the second occasion things went badly awry. You ended up staying out for 36 hours and had to be brought back. On 2nd March 2016 a referral was put in to the AMHP service in Bedford for an assessment under the Mental Health Act. This request was authorised by Dr Oluwatayo, your consultant psychiatrist, but was arbitrarily screened out by an AMHP. She decided your problems were only alcohol related. However, this person, Alida Dillon (née James), was not a qualified AMHP. She was only a 'candidate', which means she was not mandated to screen out a referral from a consultant psychiatrist without supervision from a qualified AMHP. At the inquest she said she had discussed her decision with an AMHP but there was no note of any discussion on the records. We were to encounter this candidate again, after she had qualified.

Your behaviour continued to become more and more erratic. On the Easter weekend in April, you stayed out for four consecutive nights. You ended up being taken by a paramedic to A&E in Bedford. On 8th June 2016 you jumped off a bridge in St Neots into the river. You were pulled to safety by members of the public. An ambulance was called and you were taken to A&E in nearby Hinchingbrooke Hospital. You talked to us on the phone while you were in A&E. You were terrified they would section you. In fact they were concerned about your mental health but released you back into the care of Pathway House. You were driven back to Pathway House later that evening. You didn't see any doctor, psychologist or medically qualified person, you simply went straight to bed. In the morning you got up and walked out of Pathway House, at 8.30 am, without seeing anyone. A few hours earlier, you'd attempted suicide and nobody sat down with you to talk about it. Nobody tried to stop you going. They just let you leave the premises. You were then missing for another twelve hours. The police were alerted. A helicopter was put up to search for you. You were eventually brought back and you went straight to your room. Again no qualified doctor or nurse came to see you or talk to you. You were left alone.

However, on 9th June Fiona Joyner, head of Pathway House, put in another referral to the AMHP service. It was screened out at once. On 10th June Dr Oluwatayo, incensed that the referral had been turned down, put in a further urgent referral of his own. Again inexplicably this was screened out by AMHP Patrick Moore. The consultant psychiatrist put in an immediate call to Mr Moore. The two mental health professionals then proceeded to have a massive row. The consultant psychiatrist demanded that the AMHP carry out an assessment on you. Patrick Moore refused to do so saying there was no proof an assessment was required. He claimed that more information needed to be gathered. We felt this was nonsense. You had a mental health record going back to the age of twelve and you'd just been referred by a consultant psychiatrist at a mental health clinic! The row escalated to a shouting match between two grown men and the phones were slammed down. Between the two ends of this altercation your welfare slipped through a gaping hole in the middle.

The expert witness, Dr Laurence Mynors-Wallis, is a very experienced consultant psychiatrist who specialises in anxiety disorder conditions. He has wide-ranging experience in medico-legal matters. He was an extremely impressive expert witness at your inquest. On this matter of these two requests to the AMHP being screened out, Dr Mynors-Wallace stated in court:

It is in my opinion very surprising that an assessment did not take place following the two requests for a Mental Health Act assessment in June 2016. It is my opinion that the detailed referral document should have led to a Mental Health Act assessment. I cannot recall any case in my thirty five years of clinical experience, when a detailed request for an assessment, as set out in the referral letter, would not have resulted in a MHA assessment taking place.

In the event, your needs were ignored as Patrick Moore and Dr Oluwatayo wrangled. This happened only six weeks before you died. If instead of two adult mental health professionals throwing hissy fits action had been taken, the disastrous failings in your care that followed could have been avoided.

The fourth request for an assessment was complicated and in our opinion even less excusable. After the jumping from the bridge incident you found life less and less bearable. You knew you were being moved to a new placement. One had been found but you hadn't visited it yet and you had no date for your move. As has been established uncertainty and change is anathema for most on the autistic spectrum. Milton Park is supposed to specialise in caring for people on the spectrum. They should have been aware of this and taken action. In the event they did take action but certainly not appropriate action. Fiona Joyner threatened you with eviction within 48 hours into the hands of the police. Not exactly the action of a care manager. Fiona Joyner has left Milton Park since your death. On leaving she became a beauty consultant.

Liz Hennessy, your care co-ordinator from Sussex, was now back at work. She explained in evidence to the coroner that she was very concerned about your mental state in early July. She put in the fourth request to the AMHP to come and assess you. She thought that you needed to be taken somewhere safe until your new placement was found. Liz had already located an NHS care home back in Sussex and a move was expected within weeks. But she didn't feel that the AMHP were being responsive to her request so she asked Amanda as nearest relative to take it over. Coming from your mother, Liz felt the request would have more weight. The AMHP who handled Amanda's request was the same person who as a candidate had wrongly screened out the request back in March. Alida Dillon (née James) was now mandated. She had two phone calls with Amanda. She argued strongly that you should not be assessed even for your own safety. I quote from Amanda's court witness statement:

> Alida Dillon (nee James) said to me...there is only one way this application will be made. It will be a Section 3, which means that Colette will be detained for six months. She can be sent to a facility anywhere in the country, and you her parents would have no say what so ever as to the placement.

Not surprisingly this scared us. We were very concerned about your fragile mental state at the time. We felt that if you were to be locked up, hundreds of miles away from our support, it would make you suicidal. But as we later found out from Dr Cathie O'Driscoll's Serious Incident Review (mentioned in Chapter 24), Alida Dillon (née James)'s threat was legally incorrect. Dr O'Driscoll states:

> If the assessment goes ahead and a decision is made to proceed to application under Section 3 of the Mental Health Act, the nearest relative must be consulted again.

In other words, you couldn't have been whisked away without

the AMHP consulting us, your nearest relatives, and your consultant psychiatrist would have been involved. This became clear in court under Sam Jacobs' questioning. However, back in July 2016 we withdrew our referral for the reasons stated above. We took the AMHP at her word. We feared you would be taken to a facility hundreds of miles away – we knew of similar cases where this had happened to other autistic people. This is well documented and is still happening. This misrepresentation of the facts by the AMHP was an appalling error and had tragic consequences.

Home. Where is home, I wonder?
It's not where my parents live now.
To me home is the past. A place I can feel sure about.
To every corridor there is a room. To every room a bed; a desk assigned.
Now there are no corridors. No friendly banisters dressed with the familiar garments of my family. The rooms are bereft of the golden touch familiarity offers.
I live in the past. I live it, most of the time, because my life now is robotic; meaningless. A void, without the means of navigation.
I'm lost in my actions.
My life is sparse and arid with its lack of meaning.
And I, dear and patient reader; I have made it this way!!
Why?
Because there is something in me that remains shapeless. Utterly without form or definition. I have no beginning. No middle or end. No edges; I just go round and round. Never quitting the circle but always coming back in on myself.[2]

---

2   From Colette's autobiography.

CHAPTER 27

Experts and Conclusions

By now most of the witnesses from Sussex, Milton Park and the AMHP service had given evidence and been questioned by the coroner and counsels. On the fifth day the two expert witnesses (Dr Mynors-Wallis and Marilyn Sher) read their prepared statements and were questioned. They'd had access to all the coroner's evidence. They had studied your history and the records of your diagnoses and treatment. Their reports of their findings run to 49 and 36 pages respectively. Both reports were detailed and clearly informed by wide knowledge and experience in the field of autism. They identified multiple failings in your care. I include a couple of short extracts:

From witness statement by psychiatrist Dr Mynors-Wallis
It is my opinion, however, that the team did not take account of the fact that the risks Miss McCulloch posed to herself needed to be managed whilst awaiting transfer to a different placement. She was rated as having a high risk of accident. Adequate plans were not put in place to manage the risk. Unfortunately the assessment proved to be all too accurate.

It is my opinion that the team at Pathway House failed to

put in place a management plan that was sufficiently robust to reduce the identified risks.

At the risk of repeating myself, it is my opinion that, at the point it was agreed that Miss McCulloch could no longer remain safely in Pathway House, a multi-disciplinary risk assessment meeting should have occurred, involving both Miss McCulloch and her family, the team from Sussex as well as the local team, in order to agree how best to protect her safety. This would, in my opinion, have certainly included the use of the deprivation of liberty under the Mental Capacity Act or the use of the Mental Health Act.

The use of either of these pieces of legislation could have ensured that the team had the ability to prevent Miss McCulloch from engaging in the behaviours that ultimately resulted in her death.

The second expert witness gave her evidence in the afternoon.

From witness statement by psychologist Marilyn Sher

In my opinion, an MDT multi-agency meeting would have ensured the necessary action be taken to keep her safe, whether via the MHA or MCA, as well as escalating to senior commissioners/senior people in social care.

There was clear agreement from both highly qualified professionals as to what should have been done, given your mental state. The expert witness statements were definitive. Their evidence took up one entire day of the inquest. They demolished the argument made by Milton Park that you had capacity. They tried to say that because you were a voluntary patient nothing could be done to stop you. This was not the case. There were at least three different actions that could have been taken: an assessment under the Mental Health Act, an assessment under the Mental Capacity Act or recourse to the Court of Protection. In the event, none of these actions were carried out.

It had become clear in earlier questioning of Milton Park witnesses that in the last eight weeks of your life, your psychologist, Barry Hannon, saw you just once. Your responsible clinician, Dr Oluwatayo, didn't see you at all. You received no therapy or counselling during all that time. Despite the fact that escalating risks to your life were taking place in front of their eyes, no safeguarding actions were taken. You rang us up at the end of June: 'They've given up on me, Mum and Dad – they've given up on me.'

I'm So Angry' late cartoon

In the previous days before the expert witnesses gave their evidence, Sam Jacobs had questioned Milton Park support workers and mental health professionals. He had investigated their records and found that for the last two months of your life they gave you no structured or organised activities, to fill your days – none whatsoever. They were forced to admit that was the truth. You were absolutely correct, they had washed their hands of you. They were just taking the money from Sussex Partnership Trust and waiting for you to be moved on. We bombarded Pathway House with emails over the months, asking them to keep you safe until you went to your new placement. Twelve in May and ten in June – we were incredibly worried about your safety. All these emails had zero effect.

At 8.30 am, the morning of 27th July, you left Pathway House for the last time. You had permission to be out for four hours, to visit your GP and do some shopping. Once that time had elapsed, no genuine attempt was made to get you to come back. They knew you were in a highly anxious state but they let you walk out and did nothing. Mum and I spoke to you five times that day. Our final call to you was at 9.30 pm entreating you to catch the last bus back. You ended the call abruptly. I then spoke on the phone with the support worker, Danielle Jarrett, at 9.45 pm asking her to call the police with your emergency reference code. As stated in Tracscare's Serious Incident Review:

> The police had issued Pathway House with a reference number to quote when they had concerns for CM being at risk whilst away from the residence. It gave police quicker access to records and an ability to support CM's safety more effectively.

However, for some reason Ms Jarrett didn't want to call them at that stage, despite her having been away for over twelve hours. My last call to Ms Jarrett was at 11 pm. She claims that my final call didn't take place. I know it did. I asked her once again to phone the Bedford police and report you missing.

'No, I don't want to yet. She told me she's coming back. I'll call the police at 1 am if she hasn't,' she said.

'1 am!? That's far too late Danielle!'

As I explained in the evidence I gave in court, a parent does not forget a conversation like that only hours before his daughter died. Also Amanda was with me when I talked to Ms Jarrett. There is no guarantee the police would have located you but they had on several previous occasions. There was a process in place for when you went missing. She should have followed that process in any case without our prompting. It was a well-documented procedure and the police were aware of your vulnerability. Had she acted earlier, there's a very good chance the police would have found you.

We were nearing the end of the court hearing. During the course of the inquest Sussex Partnership Trust accepted that the management of your placement at Pathway House had been inadequate and flawed. The coroner, when questioning Mr Calaminus, a new senior member of staff at East London NHS Trust (who run Bedford AMHP service), put it to him that 'the service was dire at the time'. Mr Calaminus agreed that was the case. Two out of three agencies then accepted in court that they had been seriously at fault. Not the third, however. Not Milton Park/Lakeside/Brookdale Care/Tracscare/Accomplish. Despite the evidence from the expert witnesses, they continued to maintain that you had capacity and thus it was right that they had left you to put yourself at risk. Their counsel even suggested on their behalf that:

The court should be extremely reluctant to prefer the evidence of two experts who never met Colette. They cannot be in a better position than others who knew Colette and gave evidence to the court.

The two independent expert witnesses he is referring to are eminent in their field. They would not have given evidence in court had they not been certain of what they were saying. What is more, their opinions on your lack of capacity had been established in the Complex Case Review of 2015, and as far back as by Professor Janet Treasure in 2002. These are all highly qualified and respected professionals with worldwide reputations. On the other hand, many of the Milton Park staff had no real qualifications in mental health at all. Even the psychologist Barry Hannon was not fully qualified. He was supervised by the senior psychologist, Tiago Pinto, whom we never saw and, as far as we know, you never saw. All staff were defensive throughout the inquest. Only one said he was sorry for what had happened to you. They simply stuck to saying, 'Yes she had capacity,' and we were being asked to accept their words against all evidence to the contrary.

I then gave my statement covering the history of failings in your treatment at Milton Park. I asked the coroner if I could bring the focus back onto who you were. He agreed. I read an extract from the end of a piece of prose you wrote years earlier:

So, is this the answer to breaking out?
That my arms are tied, my eyes filled with the mists of your deception.
I call it that, not because you wish to deceive, but because the colours of your perception have been mixed all wrong. To understand me, you read a book that claimed to explain all my dilemmas. You set out with the express and good intention of solving the mysteries of this over
- sensitive, high activated, CD player that picks up on all particles of dust, hindering sweet music's issue. But what

you missed, or what your blessed Bible forgot to relate,
was this one and simple rule;
I am the sum of my parts.
Without my Tape - deck, my 'stop', 'play' 'record', there is
no 'I'. No me to which definition could be given.
I am an entity bereft of that other part that makes me
function; that makes me whole.
I'm a Tea - pot without a handle.
I'll burn you when you touch.[1]

The next day, Thursday 21st March, Coroner Oldham gave his conclusion to the court. He made an initial introduction to the case. He said that after hearing all the evidence, when writing up his notes last night, he'd found himself in despair. Despair that something like this could happen in our society, in this day and age. His voice was literally cracking with emotion as he spoke. There was total silence in the court as we waited for him to read out his printed conclusion. Our experience with the coronial justice system had been, at best, mixed up until now. However, Coroner Oldham spoke from the heart as well as the head. He did not hide the fact that he was deeply upset at what had been let happen to you. It made a big difference. I will quote some key passages. He began with:

> This investigation was never about a road traffic accident because of the place where she died, a non-pedestrian area and where she was living, namely Pathway House, a mental health unit, a comparatively short distance from where she died.
>
> There has been a significant delay for which I profoundly apologise to the family and all those involved.

---

1   From 'Broken Tea-Pot' by Colette; the full text is in the Appendix.

He was referring to the two wasted years of legal wrangling with the previous coroner. He goes on to outline Dr Howard and Rebecca Simpson's comprehensive report identifying your autism in 2014. He quoted from their review:

> Colette's presentation and history is consistent with an autism spectrum disorder. This is a more helpful explanation for her presentation than personality disorder.
>
> Colette does not have the capacity to keep herself safe. It is important that staff are aware of how she plans her time and that she needs notice of appointments/activities so that she can write them into her plan.

Coroner Oldham commented that:

> The report remains in my view the most comprehensive assessment of Colette. She was a high functioning autistic young lady of talent... I have seen her art work and have read her writings and indeed Mr McCulloch her father read her prose yesterday and I suspect I shall never view a 'teapot' in the same light again. In addition to her natural talents she had taken a degree which resulted in her living in the Sussex area.

He went on to quote again from your Complex Case Review:

> She is known to experience very high anxiety, have longstanding difficulties with rituals and compulsive patterns of behaviour and be socially isolated with multiple abusive relationships. It was noted that Colette has significant executive dysfunction and generalised learning.

The report deals with her executive functioning as well as a general overview of her and is a helpful and thoughtful report. Of note is the authors' view:

> She finds too much choice overwhelming.

He put great emphasis on this issue of how choice affected you. This was encouraging as it meant he'd understood your condition and its consequences. He went on to say:

> Colette was in general terms always at significant risk of harm and this was known by all who cared for her and an immense cause of concern for her family.

He described your move to Pathway House and how your boredom and anxiety escalated. And as always when you became anxious you turned to self-medicating with alcohol. He continues with a list of disasters that took place while you were in Pathway House:

> She had a couple of home visits and then started to go to hotels close to Milton Park. Going to stop at local hotels seems incomprehensible to me, and a catalyst for disaster.
>
> If it was an aim to keep Colette safe then the move to Pathway House was a disaster. Her pattern of lifestyle changed...she drank and ended up in the River Great Ouse on 8th June 2016. Quite staggeringly she was again out missing the following day the 9th June and the Police had to instigate a search involving a helicopter.

He continued to explain what he called 'the spiral of incidents causing concern'. He commented that the acrimonious phone call between Dr Oluwatayo and AMHP Patrick Moore had resulted in:

Colette and her needs being simply swept away and were not addressed… Colette should have had proper assessment to resolve whether she should be detained under the Mental Health Act. This is I accept a draconian step but one which should have happened. It did not and Dr Mynors-Wallis told me in such circumstance he had not known, in 35 years, such a situation.

Mr Calaminus who was not in post at the time and is a senior member of staff at ELFT said: 'The focus of the trust has been to address system and procedural deficits and weaknesses that we believe created an AMHP service that was not reliably delivering high quality service.'

I agree. Colette received no service at all. Mr Calaminus was an impressive and frank witness and I put to him the service at that time was 'dire'…he agreed. The fact that there was no assessment and that the option of detaining her should have been considered and it is both a deficiency and a weakness, but it is also an acute failure on behalf of society to protect a talented but vulnerable lady.

Coroner Oldham went on to note that expert witness psychologist Marilyn Sher had commented on Milton Park giving Colette a Notice to Quit in such a brutal manner. Ms Sher said in evidence that in her view Colette:

…would have experienced this as a massive rejection as well as having instilled a sense of failure.

Martin Oldham commented that your anxiety levels in June and July seem to have considerably raised – the risks to your wellbeing were enhanced. He explored the failure of Sussex Partnership Trust and Milton Park to organise a CPA. CPA is the acronym for a Care Programme Approach. It is a framework to help assess a patient's needs. And make sure they have the necessary support. You should have had one in February. It didn't happen till the end of May. Coroner Oldham noted that this was yet another failure. He moved on to say that it was very difficult to work out from day to day what you actually did during your stay at Pathway House. He stated:

> I have spent some time looking at the Brookdale records for the period after Colette was given notice and it makes most uncomfortable reading. The records at page 468 and onwards show a disastrous situation and for the most part it is difficult to understand how Colette was being helped if at all.

He then describes the day of your death and goes on to reach his conclusion:

> Colette's death was an avoidable tragedy.
>
> I have to apply the law as stated above and have come to the conclusion regrettably that there is no direct causal connection which enables me to return a conclusion of neglect. Colette died as a result in failures for which no person directly is at fault nor any single or combination of organisations. Multiple factors and failures occurred and in the year 2019 I find this causes me considerable distress.

It caused us, her bereaved family, considerable distress as well. Neglect is the most serious conclusion a coroner can come to in a case like yours. Amanda and I are not medics or lawyers. Our legal team had sought a conclusion of 'Neglect' but had warned us that it was unlikely to be achieved, because so many different agencies and people were involved. The coroner had said earlier that:

> In broad terms there must be a sufficient level of fault to justify a finding of neglect.

So we were prepared for the ruling. However, from our layperson point of view, the Chambers Dictionary definition of the noun neglect seems correct:

> disregard; lack of (proper) care or attention, uncared-for state; negligence.

That seemed to us a pretty fair summary of the care you received during your stay at Milton Park. Nevertheless, Merry Varney and Sam Jacobs felt strongly that the coroner's conclusion of multiple failures was a strong vindication of our position, leading to the enforcement of the changes in care that we knew were necessary. Coroner Oldham's final words were ringing in our ears as we left the courtroom to give interviews to waiting journalists.

> She [Colette] was failed by the lack of a Mental Health assessment and by an inadequate regime at Milton Park which left her at large on the day of her death for far too long. No one will ever know how she came to be on the A1 but it is there she died.

CHAPTER 28

Person Centred

**Multiple failures in care of autistic
woman hit by lorry, inquest finds**
Coroner in Bedfordshire says death of Colette McCulloch was
an 'avoidable tragedy'

...was the headline of Amelia Hill's *Guardian* article reporting the
end of Colette's inquest. She went on to write later in the piece:

> ...Colette McCulloch's parents, Andy and Amanda McCulloch,
> said: 'We feel that Colette's death was predictable and preventa-
> ble. She had been displaying highly risky behaviour for months
> before her death but she was left to her own devices with no
> support, structure or activities at Pathway House.
>
> 'We repeatedly raised our concerns but these repeatedly
> fell on deaf ears. The "person-centred treatment" advertised
> by Milton Park in its brochure is certainly not what Colette
> received. We feel let down by everyone who was supposed to
> care for her and keep her safe.'
>
> They added: 'It is crucial that the failures in Colette's care
> are not swept under the carpet. It is essential that systems and
> staff are not allowed to repeat the same mistakes again.'

Deborah Coles, the director of the charity Inquest, said: 'Colette's death was predictable and preventable due to blatant failures in basic safeguarding and a series of missed opportunities.

'Colette's inquest has raised serious concerns about the treatment of women with mental ill health and autism and the need for specialist women's services. Urgent action must now be taken to ensure better monitoring and oversight of private providers of mental health services and a review of services provided to women with multiple needs.'[1]

We carried out a number of interviews for the press and TV over the next few days. Our case that Colette's death had been avoidable and was caused by negligent care was widely established. An independent Safeguarding Adult Review had also found multiple failings on the part of Sussex Partnership Trust, Milton Park and the Bedford AMHP service. Now those failings had been publicly acknowledged in a court of law. It had taken two years and eight months to reach this point. As Coroner Oldham said in court:

The Inquest lasted seven days...heard from twenty-three witnesses...saw a considerable amount of medical records.

The hours of painstaking work done by our lawyers was immense. Had that same level of resources and expertise been applied to Colette's care and treatment, she would still be alive. Our goal in pursuing this case in the coroner's court was to ensure that the same mistakes would not be made again. How could we be sure

---

1   Hill, A. (2019) 'Multiple failures in care of autistic woman hit by lorry, inquest finds.' *The Guardian*, 22 March. Accessed on 07/05/2020 at www.theguardian.com/uk-news/2019/mar/21/multiple-failures-care-autistic-woman-colette-mcculloch-hit-by-lorry-inquest-finds.

that all the promises to reform bad practice, made by the various agencies, would be carried out?

Track records of organisations acting on coroners' instructions are not good. A classic recent example being the Lakanal House Camberwell fire in 2009. The coroner listed failings that had to be addressed in any similar buildings. These were not carried through and the result was the tragedy at Grenfell.

However, the same *Guardian* article reported reassuring statements from those responsible for Colette's care and safeguarding.

Sussex Partnership Trust stated:

Following Colette's death in 2016, internal and independent investigations were held to understand how and where the NHS and other agencies failed to provide Colette with the care and support she needed. We have listened, learned and made changes to improve how we provide services as a result of this tragic incident.

Milton Park/Lakeside said:

We have changed our joint working processes to prevent an event like this happening again.

Maybe. But since the inquest we have heard nothing from Milton Park or Sussex Partnership Trust. Only the senior management from ELFT came and talked to us after the inquest. They expressed great regret at how the AMHP service had failed Colette. More importantly they said they were keen to learn from their mistakes. They asked us if we would collaborate with them on a training programme. They wanted to increase understanding in their service of how autism presents differently in women.

We agreed and a relationship has been established between us. We have been part of two successful training events on 'Autism in High Functioning Females' organised by ELFT since.

But many of the failings identified by Coroner Oldham were the responsibility of the privately run Milton Park clinic/ care home. We have received no contact from them. They were invited to send staff to the ELFT training sessions. They did not respond. Despite their reassurances that they had learned from what went wrong, the latest Care Quality Commission report on Milton Park/Lakeside does not give one confidence. Carried out in October 2019 and published in December, the report says Lakeside still requires improvement. Safety is one of the issues highlighted in this category. The CQC overall summary of Lakeside begins:

> This service was placed in special measures following the comprehensive inspection carried out in March 2018. Whilst we identified improvements during the comprehensive inspection carried out in January 2019, the provider remained in special measures due to insufficient improvement in the safe domain.[2]

So we are far from confident that the issues which contributed to Colette's avoidable death have been rigorously addressed by Lakeside. Since BBC *Panorama* uncovered the disgraceful abuse of autistic people at Winterbourne View in 2012 and Whorlton Hall in 2019, what has actually changed in the care sector? Action has been taken at those two private hospitals, of course. Staff have been fired. Clearly these hell holes should be closed down. But the real problem is that sufficient resources are not being put

---

2   CQC (2019) 'Lakeside.' Accessed on 08/05/2020 at www.cqc.org.uk/location/ 1-121852568/reports.

into mental health provision. Staff are not adequately trained. There are not nearly enough small-scale facilities available, nor is there enough care in the community. There are, as we write, over 2,000 people with autism banged up in hospitals.[3] They shouldn't be locked away like that. It is medically wrong and it is morally wrong. The grossly inhumane policies of austerity have hit the vulnerable throughout our society but the care sector has suffered most.

This brings us to an issue that must be addressed. As we acknowledged earlier, the investigations into Colette's death used up a lot of time and money. Seventy-two people died tragically in Grenfell Tower. Ninety-six died in the Hillsborough stadium disaster. In Yemen it is estimated that 85,000 children have died of starvation since 2015.[4] So why all this fuss over the death of one young woman?

The avoidable death of any child is a tragedy. We had to try and make some sense out of our daughter's death. Understanding how and why it happened is a part of that process. But that's not the full reason. We believe that her death had to be openly investigated because if just one life is swept under the bureau-cratic carpet, then all lives are devalued, and we are on a slippery slope. Already, as we have seen, our mental health services, our care systems and our NHS are all desperately underfunded. Like Colette's Tea-Pot – they are Broken. Vulnerable people, young and old, are consigned to facilities where financial profit is more important than the wellbeing of the patients. Where staff are

---

3   Hurst, G. (2019) '2,300 autistic patients are still locked up in hospital.' *The Times*, 22 March.

4   Save the Children (2018) *Yemen: 85,000 Children May Have Died from Starvation Since Start of War.* Accessed on 23/06/2020 at www.savethechildren. org/us/about-us/media-and-news/2018-press-releases/yemen-85000-children-may-have-died-from-starvation.

underpaid and undervalued. Inconvenient deaths, while in care, are covered up. It seems almost impossible in this country to access any national statistics of avoidable mortalities in state care. How long before access to medical and police records is controlled, to prevent inconvenient facts being made public, thus embarrassing vested interests? The records we finally forced out of Milton Park were redacted, chaotic and very difficult to make sense of. There were boxes and boxes of unpaginated notes, some of which did not even relate to Colette. Can you imagine how many hours it took our solicitors to sift through all that? And how much it cost?

We were lucky to meet Sara Ryan – her tenacity and courage was inspiring. She was coming to the end of her four-year campaign to get justice for her son Connor. But for her and her family's extraordinary persistence, the appalling level of care in Southern Health's mental health provision would never have been exposed. However, as I said, there are still people with autism and learning disabilities who are locked away in badly run facilities, often hundreds of miles away from where they live. Whorlton Hall and Winterbourne View are only the visible tip of a toxic mental-health iceberg. For every Colette or Connor, there are all the others whose deaths go unremarked and unnoticed. That is the reason why it is vital to fight a case like Colette's.

We were fortunate to have friends to rally round and support us in the struggle. There are too many to mention here,[5] but we owe a particular thank you to the photographer Marc Schlossman. He spent hours of his time producing our campaign video. Though none of our legal team ever met Col, they came to know her through her poems and stories and the anecdotes we told them. They aren't called *human* rights lawyers for nothing.

---

5   See the Acknowledgements at the end of the book.

What matters to them is that vulnerable people are seen as flesh and blood, people with lives that matter, not just statistics. That feeling came across in court where Coroner Oldham was visibly moved by her character, her life and her death.

CHAPTER 29

Hope...

Autumn 2019. Bright morning sun; Amanda and I walk up a tree-lined drive towards a rambling, red-brick, mock-Tudor building. This is Limpsfield Grange School for autistic girls in Oxted, just south of London. We are slightly early for our appointment with Sarah Wild the headmistress.

Much of this book has focused on what went wrong in diagnosis and treatment of Colette's mental health. Her story is a litany of failings and missed opportunities. Some were due to a lack of knowledge, including our own, about autism in women and girls at the time. Other failings were, in our opinion, caused by what we would term as 'negligence', even if they don't meet the legal definition of the word. The fact that her autism was not identified until she was thirty-three was a major factor. However, once she was diagnosed as being on the spectrum, there was almost zero care on offer for her condition of high functioning autism. What was offered was inadequate in almost every respect. Colette's case is sadly far from unique. There are no official UK figures for the number of avoidable deaths suffered by autistic people but, as can be seen in this quote from Leaders-blog by Autistic Alliance, posted 16th October 2019, the problem is huge:

The care system is broken, this had led to hundreds of hospital admissions for autistic people that could have been avoided. Over 60% of people within inpatient assessment and treatment provisions are autistic people.

How many more have been traumatised and suffered horrific or inhumane treatment, or have lost their lives? We simply cannot stand back and let this happen again. We clearly have not learnt our lesson after Winterbourne View, Mendip House and Whorlton Hall as autistic people are still suffering as a result of being placed in inappropriate long stay hospitals.[1]

Despite this bleak assessment there are some green shoots of hope. Early identification of the condition followed by appropriate care is the answer. Schools must play a vital part in this, and could prevent years of anxiety and depression for kids on the spectrum. Amanda and I visited two schools that are addressing these issues in positive ways. One is a mainstream primary school in Southwark, London. The other is a specialist girls' secondary school. So we are first going to meet Sarah at Limpsfield Grange School, Surrey.

Sarah gave us two hours of her time. She joined the school and took over as head teacher in 2012. Despite its grand surroundings Limpsfield is a state secondary school run by Surrey Education Authority. Sarah is 100% committed to the school and the pioneering work they do there, with the predominantly autistic girls, aged eleven to sixteen. She argues that keeping the school all-female makes total sense. Being overwhelmed is a huge danger for people on the spectrum. The girls don't need gender issues to be thrown at them at this age. In Sarah's opinion when

---

1   Leaders-blog, Autism Alliance (2019) 'The care system is broken.' Accessed on 08/05/2020 at www.autism-alliance.org.uk/the-care-system-is-broken.

they have meltdowns, 'autistic boys tend to explode, whereas girls implode'. Thus in mixed classes boys demand the most attention. The girls tend to go in on themselves and become isolated. Sarah told us that most girls arrive at the school stressed and exhausted by having spent years pretending to fit in and be something they are not. They need time and space to come to terms with who they are.

Limpsfield is the largest establishment in England catering for autistic girls at secondary level. The outcomes for the pupils are excellent; many going onto university or other further education. The girls come from all over southern England funded by local authorities. They come in by car or taxi from the local station. The majority are day students. There are some boarders coming from further afield. There are eighty-six pupils in total at the moment. Sadly, Sarah has to turn away more applicants than she accepts – about seven applying for each available place.

Because of the stress they may have suffered prior to admission, some pupils may have learned a variety of antisocial behaviours. Sarah explained that autistic girls are very prone to copying self-destructive behaviours and adopting them. Often girls will already have developed other conditions like OCD. There are a number of neuro-diverse pupils who have several conditions. These have to be taken into account when working with the pupils. But the predominant condition is Autistic Spectrum Disorder, though Sarah Wild prefers the term Autistic Spectrum Continuum. The school does not see autism as being a disorder. Most pupils nowadays have been identified as being on the spectrum before they arrive at Limpsfield.

The school teaches ABC: Action, Behaviour, Consequences. Something autistic girls find hard to understand and have to be taught. Boundaries are very important for girls on the spectrum. They have to learn what is and what is not acceptable behaviour.

Boundaries must be upheld. They require certainty, not confusion. Autistic girls are often in a state of anxiety. If they go to university it is advisable to go to one where they can live at home. Dealing with living away and studying can be overwhelming. Too many social pressures. Later in life some girls may be able to manage a job and a relationship, others may find that too much to deal with and have to choose one or the other.

We met two pupils. They were engaging and very bright; one bubbly, the other more reserved. When Amanda asked the bubbly one how she felt when she first arrived, she replied: 'Oh it was amazing, I mean there were other girls like me – I mean sort of like me. I thought I'd be alone all my life, but now I know I won't be any more.'

The school grounds are spacious and there are many animals, dogs, cats, hamsters, etc. there for them to look after. They really like this and value the animals. The whole place had a warm, friendly feeling. But it's apparent as we talk with Sarah Wild that if more primary schools identified autistic girls and gave them help, much mental pain and distress could be avoided. Early identification is the key. Our next port of call is such a school...

Bessemer Grange Primary School, Herne Hill, Southwark, consists of two modern buildings. The early years section is housed in a low-rise structure with plenty of natural light coming from the many windows. This is where Jodi Charman and her team work, with mainly autistic kids.

Jodi is a charismatic Australian with infectious cheerful energy and commitment. She's worked her way from being a children's hairdresser, to become first a classroom assistant, then to specialise in teaching kids with learning difficulties and autism. While doing this she has gained a number of qualifications in subjects ranging from using Makaton (a form of sign language) to understanding Applied Behaviour Analysis. She oversees the class provision and lesson differentiation for children with SEND (Special Education Needs and Disability) in the school, as well as running numerous specialist interventions. She has become a vital member of Bessemer School staff. Her job title now is: SEND/EHCP Coordinator.

Pupils have to be identified by staff before being assessed for autism and learning difficulties. If teachers think a pupil may have ARD (Autism Related Disorder) Jodi, or one of her team, is called in. Jodi will then collect evidence through a process of observations and assessments. The Head of Inclusion, another staff member, will then request an assessment by a Paediatrician at Sunshine House, the Children and Young People's Developmental Centre in Camberwell. If the assessment diagnoses autism or learning disabilities this will release funding for the child.

This process of 'identifying' kids on the spectrum often happens in nursery school or reception class. The earlier pupils are identified the better. More boys are identified than girls, though that gap is narrowing according to Jodi. Parents sometimes have difficulties in accepting a diagnosis of autism. They experience grief. They feel there is a stigma attached to the label. However, they soon learn that there can be positive aspects to the condition. Many autistic children are talented, and yes, they do see the world through different eyes. But their unique view is often insightful and creative. And there are extraordinary people ranging from Albert Einstein to Greta Thunberg, from Emily Dickinson to Wolfgang Amadeus Mozart, from Chris Packham to Susan Boyle who are or were on the spectrum. Jodi makes it clear to parents that their children have real potential but they do need support. She finds that the kids soon respond to the individual care and progress well.

Jodi took us first to her 'satellite' room. Pupils have 'one to ones' there. The walls are uncluttered and white. Strong colours, images and noise can be very disturbing. Then she took us through a number of classes where these kids were learning alongside neuro-typical children but with extra assistance from a trained adult. Picture Exchange Communication System (PECS) and Communicate in Print are used to help them talk, read and understand. By associating pictures with the words, one by one, they start to read. It takes time but the responses are amazing. Kids who were non-verbal are soon learning to talk, read and write. Some kids relate strongly to one teacher or assistant. If they can't see that person, they can get very anxious. Sometimes just holding a piece of the teacher's clothing will reassure them. If a child has a meltdown they will be taken to the 'Sensory Room'. This is a very calm place. There are soft lights. There is low music. They can sit on a cushion, inside a circle of long ribbons. Then when they are ready they are quietly taken back to their class.

The atmosphere in the classrooms is positive throughout. Up to twenty-three kids in this school of six-hundred are cared for by this team. Other schools of this size have identified no autistic students at all. There is no way that can be right. Clearly many primary schools without Bessemer's expertise are letting young autistic kids slip through the net. Most kids from Bessemer will go on to mainstream secondary schools, Jodi tells us. Some may require additional support. A small minority with severe difficulties may move on to special schools.

These two schools in the state sector, one primary, one secondary, are achieving amazing outcomes for their pupils. There are other examples in the UK but far too few. I estimate, given the under-diagnosis of females, that there are at least a million people on the spectrum in the UK, and 25% of those will be children. That means a quarter of a million kids who are struggling to cope.

These schools show that autistic people can and do flourish in the right circumstances. We need more Bessemer and Limpsfield Granges, so as to unlock the potential of these young people.

CHAPTER 30

Beginning

Wednesday 8th April 1981. I drove up to St Thomas's Hospital, on the South Bank of the Thames, to take a very pregnant Amanda into the obstetrics ward. You were late. The due date for your arrival into this world had passed ten days ago. In the last few days, you'd stopped growing. The medics weren't happy. A decision had been made to induce you out from the comfort of your mother's womb. (It seems that you were fearful of change even back then.) We got there at 4 pm. Amanda went into the ward while I parked the car in a street nearby.

I was back in the ward with Amanda when they gave her the injection to induce her labour. By 10 pm nothing was happening. I went out to get something to eat. By the time I got back a nurse asked me to come through quickly to the delivery room. Amanda's waters had broken. The nurses were reassuring. They put a hospital gown on me. The contractions were coming regularly. Amanda was dilating but not enough yet. You were stubbornly resisting. The obstetrics doctor, looking increasingly tired, came in every 15 minutes or so, in his surgical wellie boots, making encouraging noises. But you were still hanging back. It was now about 2.30 am. The doctor said he would have to use forceps to deliver you. Amanda was alarmed. Chloe had been a forceps delivery and she had needed a lot of stitches afterwards. He told her not to worry, forceps were much improved since five years ago!

He regarded me with world-weary eyes and suggested I might prefer to go out at this point. However, he took in that I was reluctant to leave Amanda. He shrugged and said, 'Well so long as you're not squeamish, stay and be useful, encourage your wife.'

'Oh that's not a problem. I used to help my dad deliver the calves on the farm.'

He gave me what I took to be a withering look and set about his work. Amanda pushed and pushed with cries of frustration. I tried to encourage her: 'Come on love, push, push.'

'I'm not a bloody cow!' she yelled, eyes flashing.

The Jamaican midwife/nurse smiled across to me. She'd seen it all before. Then, in what seemed to me a blur of minutes, you were pulled out. The nurse expertly took you from the doctor and his forceps. Your umbilical cord was cut. She slapped you professionally on the back – once, twice. You shouted out a whopping cry of life. I looked round; even the nurses were moist eyed. I realised that I had tears in my eyes too. Amanda lay back on the bed, exhausted. We held hands briefly before the nurse passed you to Amanda and everybody left us for a moment.

We sat there in the now-quiet birthing room, the three of us. Amanda lay in bed, propped up by pillows. I held you. You were so small and vulnerable. I was terrified of dropping you. I passed you back to your mum. I was suddenly very hungry.

'I brought some of your spinach quiche with me, would you like a piece?'

She gave me an old-fashioned look... 'I think a cup of tea might be nice. My hands are quite full at the moment.'

She gazed at you. 'It's incredible – she looks so like

Chloe.' There was a family likeness but you were to be a very different baby.

I drove to collect you and Amanda a few days later. Chloe came with me. She was five years old, just starting school. You lay in the back of the car in your carrycot. Your mum one side, Chloe the other. She regarded you in wonder and gently stroked your head. We set off for home.

From Colette's autobiography:

Do I really intend this manuscript of my brief life to be published? Would I want the people I know and love to read exactly how I have felt; how I have construed certain events and passages in time? Do I want people to read about themselves? Most importantly, however, do I stand a chance of becoming a writer, a novelist, as I have always wanted to be?

And if this were to be published; to appear in the wisdom of the printed word, would it help anyone else that has ever struggled with the concept of living, of surviving, of finding ways to cope and get through in a world that seems perpetually demanding. Could it help anyone that has ever suffered?

I hope so.

Colette

For Colette

Des McAleer, August 2016

To think we once took such gifts as givens,
The infant instinctively would suckle, grip,
And parental worry subside to oversee

Our kin and kith independently thrive.
In the odd case something went wrong
There'd be provision in the system, so rich
In its diagnostic lexicon.
I was your overnight guest, chance had brought
To intrude on grief for your daughter's death.
She might have missed the last departing bus;
Or an unlicensed cabbie mistook the turn
Dropping her off on the opposite side.
The officer conjectured that her wavy walk
Strayed into the path of a juggernaut.
And what could redeem her anorexic youth?
The waivered years lost as a famine waif.
Once too often she left the treatment centre
For a night on the town, at thirty-five
Still keeping faith in the romantic encounter.
We'd talk of education, a change of career,
While she dreamed of weeks in Magaluf.
Our dream is shrivelled flowers, a roadside shrine,
A concrete hard-shoulder, and momentarily
Tagging featureless space, a date and name.
Where traffic hurtles, so relentless no well-
Intentioned chauffeur will chance pulling over
For the benighted straggler, astray on the verge,
Out too late, and lacking all sense of the time.

Acknowledgements

This deserves more prominence than coming at the end of this tome. However, they make more sense once you've read it. I can hear you shouting at me, 'Get on with it Dad, just write it!' That's what you did. Simply banged the words down, almost never rewriting at all. You had a point; I need to get on with it. Here we go.

First of all there's our family who have stuck by us and supported us, through the years. Firstly your older sister Chloe, her partner Teddy and their three much-loved, life-affirming children Ollie, Sam and Amy. The strength of their love and their little family has been our rock. Then my nephew Nick, who was very close to you, and my brother Patrick and his family. They helped hold us together in the darkest hours of grief. They all brought humour and perspective back into our lives. They helped us talk about you, relating tales of all your weird and wonderful ways.

Then friends – there are too many to name. However, here are a few to whom we owe an enormous debt – Caroline and Edmond O'Reilly whose Brighton home was a refuge for us. Jim and Valerie Evans who lent you money and rescued you when you'd lost your keys. Puck Gibbs and Ursula Jones who always thought you were special and told you so. Jan Evans, your mum's closest friend, your non-godmother, who is the best listener in the world. Michael Carter who talked to you and helped you in getting into rehab. James Woolley and Mike Grady who resolutely supported us in our CrowdJustice campaign. And locally, in south-east London, our near neighbours, Meryl and Chris Heron and Penny and Giles Block. They cooked delicious meals for us, cheered us up and were always there for us.

Then from days in the Bethlem Royal Hospital, Prof Janet Treasure and nurses Gill Todd and Norma Patterson as well as patients Caz Spray and Gemma King were hugely important in your life.

In our campaign to achieve justice for you and get your story out there, Gerard Panting, Sara Ryan and George Julian came into our lives and showed us a way through the daunting labyrinth of the English coronial system. Without their help we wouldn't have got to base camp. Gerard in particular led us to the formidable armies of Leigh Day and Doughty Street Chambers, made up of Merry Varney, Dan Webster, Caoilfhionn Gallagher QC and barrister Sam Jacobs. They were humane and forensic, encouraging us when we were in despair and bulldozing the path through what seemed to be a series of impossible obstacles, to find justice. We owe them a huge debt of gratitude. They never wavered in their belief in our case.

We are enormously grateful to the CrowdJustice team who worked hard for our campaign. And to the #JusticeforCol supporters, most of whom we don't know, but whose commitment and generosity enabled the campaign to succeed. Without them, we would never have achieved a full and open inquest into your avoidable death.

A special thanks must go to friends Roger Davenport, Brigitte Lardinois and Des McAleer for ploughing through, and commenting on, the chapters as I shovelled them out of my laptop. Theirs was support that went far beyond the call of mere friendship. Their insights and corrections were invaluable.

We want to thank Sarah Hamlin, Vicki Peters and the team at Jessica Kingsley Publishers, for leading us through the mysteries of publishing a book for the first time.

Finally, our thanks must go to two people who played vital roles in our campaign #JusticeforCol: Jane Asher, president of the National Autistic Society, and photographer Marc Schlossman. Jane spoke movingly in our campaign video, and later took the time and trouble to read this book and write an empathetic and intuitive foreword. Marc shot and edited your video. With great care he photographed all the images of your work that appear in this book. Throughout he has supported us and even shared the odd glass of Islay malt whisky with me.

Appendix

Complete text of three pivotal poems by Colette.

Note to my Parents

Would you believe me
If I said that life has become
Impossible?
That your daughter feels she cannot
Breathe the very air around her.
That, to run a bath and wash
Is too much effort of a will
lost looking at a hat
In the window of a pink shop.
Would you believe me
If I told you that I deliberately
Do what I don't want to
Just to see how far it goes.
That I'm bleeding in the mirror
Daily now. Like before,
But deeper.

A scoop of scalp to rest my pain in.
Black nails at Breakfast.
Little moons of crusted blood
In the sink I haven't cleaned
Since doomsday.
Blood's metal smell
Strange comfort.
Why?
I listen to you
In the kitchen;
A crouching toad of thought.
Muttering mice,
You whisper like the kids at school,
But I confess there is concern
Etched on the faces of you both,
As I crouch and learn your mind of me.
Forbidden chocolate,
Because I wet the bed in guilt.
A lake of off-milk yellow
Drawn around in cadbury's pen.
This is me;
My human stain.
Remember?
Remember, Dad,
Those few days spent together.
Mum's voice hidden in the telephone.
A heart and land away from here.
And then, when she returned,
I turned six again and wet the bed
When for days I'd kept the flood
At bay. Why?
Some bitter revenge

To strike and say
It's all her fault I'm young.
Because I look at her
And see a crumbling wall I stamp on,
Still,
My gypsy boots intact.
Rumplestiltskin with a mask.
Greedy fingered need to be loved
Without my loving.
There's little left of her.
A pile of bricks tilting for want of cement.
Dad?
You make me hate myself
With all your open-wound suffering;
An exhibition of tears.
If only I were Alice
I might drown away
down the river of mum's spine
To the womb I never really left.
You make me hate myself.
It's like Mozart's Requiem;
my tidal pain.
You think I don't realise
your suffering, but I live it;
Just for you.
I pretend, I act,
I dress myself in the clothes
I saw a young girl wearing,
Wishing I was her,
But wishing bubbles.
Pop!
Tic, tic, tic of a mind

Never letting go to being.
So simple.
So simply hard.
There's no reality
Save what you make of it, and mine goes tic, tic, tic.
An itch my severed arms can't reach to.
Sunday afternoons
Before the dreaded Monday;
The sinking of a boat on weekend waters.
I always felt that boat, the sink,
on Sunday afternoons.
Scabs start forming
On my skin
and I feel I'm juxtaposed.
Many reflections.
Different perspectives.
My God, so that is how
They see me.
A profile of lies.
My heads bleeding the memories;
Fish fingers on toast,
The dog we had who was
A person; His seal head and loo-roll snout.
Chimmey. An echo in the red tiled kitchen.
The only labrador
With a curly tail.
A smile of swaying black
Becoming a dot in the green of my mind.
He was me.
I was him.
Mongrel mixed race breed.
Apparently they don't make them anymore.

Shelf-objects

28th December 2003

Strange-scented mornings;
Peace of mind on Saturdays.
The clock ticking comfort
On a shelf
Above the bed, or was it
Near the window?
Memories I thought would
Never fade
Have seeped into a quiet
Seapier.
The handle of the kitchen door
Leading to the garden
Had a special quality,
A character childhood
Invests in the material.
How can I say
That certain objects,
Things became a person,
Entity? They had a life.
The teddies having
Picnics while we slept,
And quickly sitting down
Before we had a chance
To see the magic. But we
Were sure it happened,
Just as our droopy
Eye-lids closed.
Pink glow of Autumn,

Wellingtons and Piles
Of leaves. Orange Streets
And conckers.
Mum wore picksy boots
With pointy toes
And laces. Too much
Eye-line even then.
A tiny wrinkled hand
In mine; 'Kitchen Hands'
She always said,
And I laughed, never
Thinking I would one day
Have the same,
And at a younger age.
I'd press the ball of
Her thumb, feel the
Hardened skin collapse
Beneath my pressure;
Like air-pop wrapping
Used for delicate things;
Like mum.

Always the same
Burnt hot-chocolate-croissant
On a Sunday; the pastry
Cracking between
Milk white rabbit teeth;
A front-gap to stick my tongue between
I'd curl in warmth
With the dog, our dog;
A member of the family.
The other man in the house

Hovering between all these
Women
Long golden afternoons
In summer with friends
I'd barely recognise now.

Broken Tea-Pot

There is no reality save what is real in yourself.
To some this place could offer sanctuary; a place to
　　continue self-destruction within the confines of
　　seeming safety. It could be an excuse to hate all
　　the more those that exert pressure and their own
　　will upon you. Homeless, it might provide shelter.
　　And, one cannot negate the seductive powers of
　　having busy - bodies involved in our care 'ME'. ME.
　　ME!!!!' our hollow eyes will hoarsely scream across a
　　table, a barrier that separates us from them.

But now, for me, and at this moment my reality is this;
A bottomless pit of questions without answers. Voices
　　in my wake and in my sleep, the latter an echo of
　　what took place before.
The long march to the front lines, to fight the war with
　　food. My enemy and my dearest friend. My denial
　　of you created my love for you; what have I to
　　cling and love now?
To wake up with the sheets wet and clinging; another
　　film of skin. The flesh piles up.
Numb with useless fear and foreboding, my days
　　form eternities of silent horror.

What am I doing?! How the hell will I get back to what I was before.

I'm jelly in their hands. Unable to support myself, they go by the text book on how to make me firm and solid; a solidification of what they believe.

To muse upon these feelings is like drinking coffee that's continuously topped - up with water: you lose the sense of the initial taste of thought; the thing that made you write in the first place. It becomes a boring rendition of all the clichés you've ever heard, plus more for dramatic effect.

I remember once hearing someone say; (I forget who) that to make 'Art' out of the Holocaust was profanity in the extreme. To try and encapture, or represent something so inhuman, so atrocious beyond words would be suggesting that such a level of unthinkable suffering was in some ways beneficial. Take this a few steps further, it would be saying that suffering of this kind was 'good' for the human spirit to learn from, and to emulate regarding endurance in their own trifling ways. In a sense it could be perceived as paradigmatic. As in science, one set of beliefs is replaced by the new. Thus the scientist learns from the mistakes and successes of the former.

In the same way; (though to a much lesser extent), it is profane of me to attempt at describing in mere words what my mind currently endures. Words

nor images do justice to the brutality of this
experience.

But here I sit, my fingers laboriously drumming this
  key - board, trying to do poetic justice to what I
  think I'm feeling; or what I think I think.
To bleed myself of mental pain; replace it with a
  physical ailment to which others would respond
  with predictable sympathy.

I've lost an arm, a limb. Would you believe me when I
  told you this was just as bad? Do people get used
  to not having something they've had since they can
  remember. Does it cease to hurt that everything,
  no matter how precious, is transient; ephemeral as
  the smooth milk skin of the new - born babe. We
  are all leaves that fall, and wrinkle with the season's
  change.

It's not fair, I want to scream, that I can't continue this
  existence and attain the happiness of my heart.
It's not fair that, though my life at present is as limited
  as the cage we bar wild tigers in, life outside these
  bars feels commensurably worse.
The Devil you know. The pain I'm now used to.

So, is this the answer to breaking out?
That my arms are tied, my eyes filled with the mists
  of your deception.
I call it that, not because you wish to deceive, but
  because the colours of your perception have been
  mixed all wrong. To understand me, you read a

book that claimed to explain all my dilemmas. You set out with the express and good intention of solving the mysteries of this over - sensitive, high activated CD player that picks up on all particles of dust, hindering sweet music's issue. But what you missed, or what your blessed Bible forgot to relate, was this one and simple rule;

I am the sum of my parts.

Without my Tape - deck, my 'stop', 'play' 'record', there is no 'I'. No me to which definition could be given.

I am an entity bereft of that other part that makes me function; that makes me whole.

I'm a Tea - pot without a handle.

I'll burn you when you touch.